RICH FRIEND POOR FRIEND

Leave A Legacy! It Cost ZERO Dollars To Think Link A Millionaire

By
Moe Evans

© Copyright 2020 by Maurice Evans - All rights reserved.

It is not legal to reproduce, duplicate, or transmit any part of this document in either electronic means or printed format. Recording of this publication is strictly prohibited.

ISBN-9798556041523

PRINTED IN THE UNITED STATES OF AMERICA

Contents

Contents iii

Preface 1

My Personal Story 3

My Rich Friend and Poor Friend 88

The 4 Essential Wealth Skills 117

7 Key Ways to Change Tomorrow, Today 140

Making Money Online For Beginners 163

LIMITS OF LIABILITY / DISCLAIMER OF WARRANTY:
The Author has strived to be as accurate and complete as possible in the creation of this book, notwithstanding the fact that he does not warrant or represent at any time that the contents within are accurate due to the rapidly changing nature of the Internet.

While all attempts have been made to verify information provided in this publication, the Author assume no responsibility for errors, omissions, or contrary interpretation of the subject matter herein. Any perceived slights of specific persons, peoples, or organizations are unintentional.

There are no guarantees of income made. Readers are cautioned to rely on their own judgment about their individual circumstances to act accordingly. This book is not intended for use as a source of legal, business, accounting or financial advice. All readers are advised to seek services of competent professionals in legal, business, accounting, and finance field.

Screen shots seen in this manual are from publicly accessible files and web pages and used as "fair use" for reporting purposes and to illustrate various points mentioned herein. Texts and images available over the Internet may be subject to copyright and other intellectual rights owned by third parties.

DEDICATION

I dedicate this book to my Great Grandfather and ALL of his offspring.

All he brought to the United States from The Virgin Islands was his last name and courage. A former Baltimore Black Sox player…… LEGACY

And to my Brother who introduced me to THE HUSTLE!

Preface

This is not your ordinary book. It is broken down into three sections to give my reflections on my journey to become a "Rich Friend". These are personal stories in my life to only reflect the length of the journey. There is no mention of names as this is only part, a reflection. Once becoming a "Rich Friend" the journey does not stop there.

Inspired by Robert Kiyosaki and his book "Rich Dad Poor Dad" this book brings a unique perspective from the eyes of a young man just trying to create his own lane. When you really look at it, most success stories took a long time to develop. This is no different.

I wrote this book in hopes to assist people to see things differently. Thoughts become habits, habits become behavior, behavior becomes character, character leaves a legacy. Leave something for your kid's kid's kids.

Covid 19 has affected so many. This book gives a tiny fraction of the opportunities available in the world. I give indirect ways that anyone can start making money in the last section of the book. I hope it sparks a new idea in every reader.

"An Idea is the seed that blossoms to <u>FRUIT</u>ion"

Moe Evans

My Personal Story

Marketing has been instilled in me before I even knew what marketing was. The thing was, I was always marketing my own business, that is why it didn't seem like marketing.

The first time I marketed for my own business, my business was a service. Any business must have a service or a product, if it doesn't, then it is an illegal business (Ponzi).

It was winter 1988. I was 8 years old. A snowstorm blew through the Baltimore, Maryland region and dropped about 4 to 5 inches of fluffy white snow! My older brother who was 12 years old at the time, came home extra excited (AFTER the streetlights came on, but really like 7p.m, it gets dark early in the winter).

"Boy where the hell you been?" I remember my dad yelling as my brother walked through the door. My pops, a military veteran, did not play any games when it came to being a parent. He stood there with his hands on his hips with his head cocked to the left towering over my shivering brother.

My brother was shivering because he was cold, not because he was in fear. The only reason I could tell was because he still had that silly looking grin on his face as his lip trembled.

He kind of stuttered or mumbled the first time he tried to respond. He was being extra dramatic to help ease the tension in the air. This immediately got my mother's attention.

"Boy What?.....Slow down!......Take those wet clothes off and have a seat. Let me make you some hot chocolate" my mother interjected.

All the teeth chattering, and extra shivering seemed to immediately cease, and before he could get his second boot off, he blurts out again, but with a much clearer voice, "I made 74 dollars shoveling snow! I would have been home sooner, but I convinced this lady to let me shovel her back patio for her dog, for an extra 7 bucks!"(UpSell)

As he slides out of his dungarees that were wet from the cuff up halfway his calf, he pulls out a wad of money folded exactly in half and brings it to the table and has a seat.

"Where were you at shoveling?" I remember my dad asking. The question was one of concern, and it was written all over his face. When my brother told him where he was shoveling, my father put his hand on my brother's shoulder and said "please please please be safe out there. I don't want you out there when it's dark like this either". My brother agreed while he sat at the table loudly counting his earnings for the day.

You would have thought from the tone of my father's voice that we lived in a crime infested neighborhood filled with gangs, drugs and violence. But that was the furthest thing from the truth. We lived in a quiet semi-rural section of Baltimore County where you rarely hear of any kind of murders or stuff like that.

What my father feared back in 1988, was our safety when roaming through and around white people. Although the town we lived in was not plagued with drugs and crime, it was indeed infected with racism.

It was a highly segregated town and my brother had already experienced an incident when swimming at his buddy's grandma's house. She screamed out the back door "Get that nigger out of my pool!". My brother's buddy stood up for him and they finished swimming that day.

Any who………..

All I could think about was how I was going to spend his money. (LOL)

Indeed, I was about to get the Nintendo robot and Mike Tyson Power glove along with a new remote-control car, with HIS MONEY.

Or so I thought.

My brother taught me 2 of the MOST VALUABLE lessons I have learned in life that day.

1.) You Have To Go And Get It
2.) You Have To Go And Get It To Go And Get It

And this is how my Marketing Career truly began!

The very next day, in the late afternoon, while the sun was bright and slowly melting the white gold away, I decided to go make my own money. I took the only shovel we had, which was a heavy square metal shovel with a heavy duty 5 ft long wooden handle.

The metal head of the shovel was completely rusted, and the long wooden handle was smooth and heavy. I remember dragging it behind me as I walked the streets trying to find a customer.

I stayed away from the area my dad told my brother to stay away from and ventured toward the elementary school I was attending. As I walk, I notice that most of the homes had already had their driveways and sidewalks shoveled. Still I moped around knocking on any door who had not had their snow cleared.

After about an hour or two of walking with no luck, I decided to head back home. It was starting to get dark and I was cold.

2 Blocks away from my house, I spot a car pulling into their un-shoveled driveway. This is my last hope to make some money.

As I approach the house a white lady much older than my mother slowly opened her car door and braced herself in the snow to keep her balance from slipping. I shout out, "I can clear that snow for you right quick, so you don't have to worry about slipping and falling".

She looks at me puts one hand on her hip and says with a disgruntle tone "my nephew was supposed to come by and do this yesterday. He never showed up. How much are you going to charge me Hon'?"

My eyes got big; my stomach filled with butterflies. I got through my pitch now it's time to close the deal. I didn't want to go too high and scare her off, but I didn't want to hesitate like this was my first rodeo.

I blurt out "10 bucks!".

She looks at me and says "oh heavens no! This little bit of snow will probably melt before the next time I come out."

I blew it! I went too high! She was scared off, already turning her body toward her front door away from my direction. I could not give up that easy though. Instead of lowering my price, I did for the first time, what ALL GREAT salespeople do. I "created a problem".

"Well ma'am, I will do your driveway, your walkway to your driveway, your steps, and I will even do your front sidewalk, so when other people walk in front of your house, they don't have to worry about slipping" I hurry up and say before she reaches her top porch step.

She reached for her porch railing, turned all the way around to face me as I stood all the way at the foot of her driveway. She firmly placed her fist, gripping an enormous set of keys, into her side. I remember hearing the keys jingle and then a moment of silence.

"I tell you what hon', you do all of that and do a good job and I will pay you 5 dollars plus a tip. How does that sound?" she said after taking a deep long exhale.

I immediately stand the shovel that I was dragging, straight up, and say "DEAL!"

I start on her front sidewalk and start where her neighbor's already cleared sidewalk stopped. After knocking her sidewalk out, I did the driveway, then the sidewalk from the steps to the driveway and last the steps.

After only about 15 minutes of labor, I was done. I rang the doorbell, and the lady came to the door surprised.

"Done ALREADY?" she exclaimed as she opened the screen door and only stuck her head out, to look at my job. When the door opened, I was hit dead in the face with a thick warm delightful aroma of something baking. I remember looking at her toes, slightly hanging over the doorway step, painted in a vibrant red nail polish and then up to her eyes and reply "Yes ma'am".

She scanned over her walkways and driveway and then her steps.

"Ok hon', looks good to me. Give me a second, I'll be right back" she responded.

I lean the shovel up against her railing and start to think of what I was going to spend my money on. Chips, ice cream, soda, cake. In that order. Not quite the same selection that an 8-year-old has today. I probably would have wanted to go to the dollar store or 5 below, if we had that back then.

After only a minute or two of thought into what I was going to purchase, the lady comes back, still tucked away in her flannel robe, lips matching her toes. In her left hand I see three bills and in her right hand, at first, I could not see exactly what it was because her hand was partially behind the door.

"Here you go hon" she says reaching out the 3 bills. 5 Dollars for the job and 2 dollars for a tip" she says.

I reach out and grab the money and thank her and the she shuffles a Styrofoam cup, topped with steam that was blowing back into her house, from her right hand to her left and says "and here is some hot chocolate" then she shuffles a Ziplock sandwich bag into her hand as well and says "and here are some homemade chocolate chip M&M cookies".

Extra excited, I thank her again and grab the hot chocolate and the bag with the 2 cookies.

She said "you're welcome hon" and went back in the house. I stood there on her freshly shoveled porch for a few minutes and sipped my hot chocolate. Halfway through the cup I thought about my dad, and his fear of white people. What if she put poison in the hot chocolate, what about the cookies? I clearly remember these thoughts running through my head, then I quickly dismissed those thoughts, and I devoured those delicious cookies.

They were still warm when she gave them to me as some of the chocolate had smeared on the clear Ziplock bag. After finishing the hot chocolate and cookies right there on her steps, I put the cup in the bag, grabbed my shovel with the other hand and dragged it all the way home.

So, my first earned income was in 1988. I did my own marketing, door to door, I made the sale for a service, and then I rendered the service and got paid.

Every winter there after I would PRAY for snow. When I was 14, I decided to make my first business card. I had a printer, so I just printed my info into business card size pieces of paper and left them at neighbor's houses.

Shoveling snow also ventured out to raking leaves and cutting grass. It takes a lot of confidence to go to stranger's doors and solicit services, but by starting at the age of 8 I fine-tuned the skill of door to door sales early.

Although, every season seemed to bring some sort of business, I always had to wait. I had to wait for it to snow. Some winters may have only brought 2 snowstorms. Had to wait for people's grass to grow. That door to door business was reliant on outside factors.

But as a kid, an extra pair of tennis shoes every season, maybe a few pair in the winter, always seemed like it was worth the wait.

This door knocking experience would carry me into my adulthood. This was the cornerstone of my marketing career……..

SON OF A COACH.....

Being the son of a coach has its advantages as well as its disadvantages. I played football, baseball, basketball and even lacrosse. Football was my main sport though.

My father was my head coach for a couple of my teams but was my permanent coach at home. Without his guidance I'm sure I would have never become a Quarterback. He always demanded me to be the smartest player on the team. I might not have been the most athletic, but whatever I lacked athletically, I made up for it mentally.

He made me pay attention to the details. Any time a toy or a new game was brought in the house, if it had directions, he forced me to read them. There was no "just try and figure it out". Directions are clear cut. If you can read, there is no excuse for not reading and following the directions.

Being a quarterback only enhanced my confidence as a person. The quarterback is the most important position in football and is automatically designated as a leader. Taking on that leadership role deposited mental toughness that I would need in the future.

My football career came to an abrupt halt after graduating High School. I did attend Marshall University as a walk-on recruit but was immediately turned away when they said that they never received my Clearinghouse paperwork. This is the paperwork that is needed to show you are academically eligible to play collegiate sports.

The sad part is, my SAT score (1130) and my GPA(3.5) was clearly above the eligibility criteria to play. I automatically assumed that my High School guidance counsellor took care of it but she did not.

This was one year after Hall of Fame Wide Receiver Randy Moss left. This was also former NFL quarterback Chad Pennington's last year at Marshall University and the first year for former NFL Quarterback and present-day (2020) Offensive Coordinator for the Tampa Bay Buccaneers, Byron Leftwich.

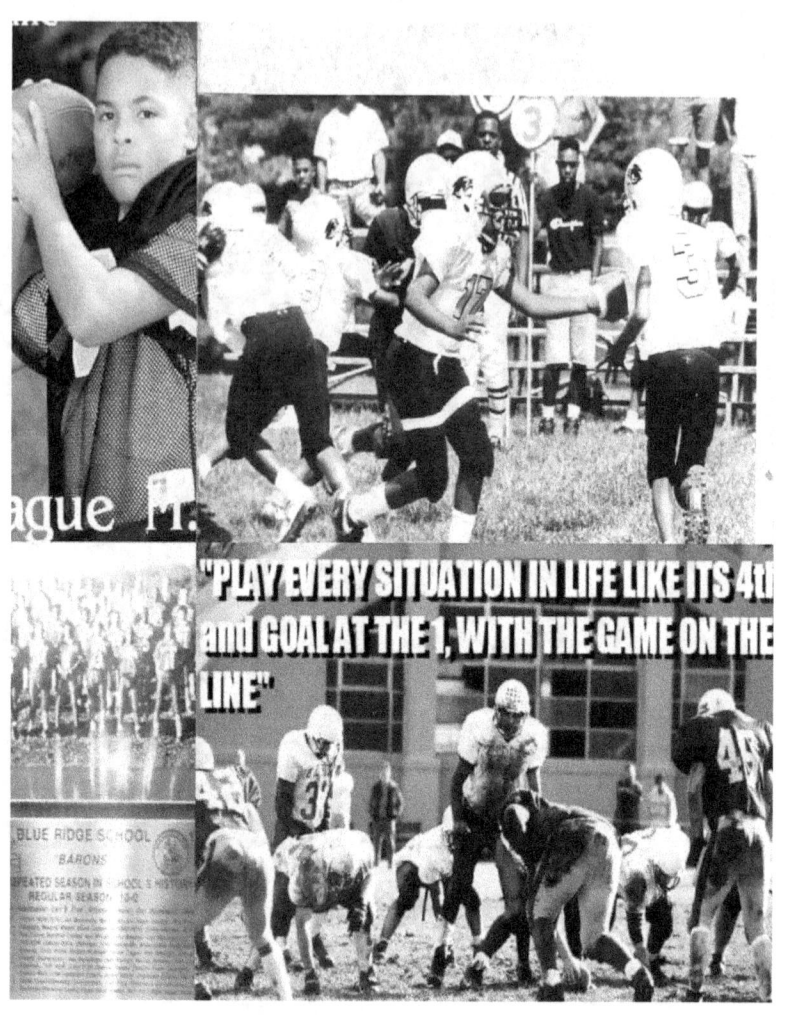

FOOTBALL IS DONE!

Growing up, I never really concentrated on being anything in particular. I played sports and got good grades. That's it! Not a doctor, not a lawyer, teacher, nothing.

Football afforded me the opportunity to attend a Private High School out of state. My Senior year, I led my team to the School's FIRST Undefeated Regular Season in the School's history! One of the Oldest Remaining all boys boarding schools in America. We left a Plaque on the wall FOREVER!

The guidance counsellor at that same school though, failed to submit my paperwork for my football career to continue. I will never forget the feeling I had when I went to the Fieldhouse at Marshall University on check-in day.

It was a line of guys all checking in for the football team. When I got to the front of the line, the guy asks my name, looks over a list like we are at a VIP Party, then looks at me and says "Sorry son, we don't have your Clearinghouse paperwork. You can't even put on a jockstrap without that!". He gave a little chuckle then hollered "NEXT!"

I turned around to leave but couldn't help but notice some of the guys getting a good chuckle in as well. My stomach immediately went sour and I began to feel really nauseous. The walk from the fieldhouse to my room was the longest mile I have ever walked in my life. I was lost. Hundreds of miles away from home, before the fall semester (August 1998) even started and football was over.

I finished that freshman year at Marshall but came back home to Baltimore after the spring semester. (May 1999) Felt like the biggest disappointment ever. My parents were going through their divorce that school year, and my pops would also find someone else. My Grandmother passed away that school year as well. My Mom's mother. Her funeral was in Jacksonville, Florida and just so happened to be during my winter break.

I'm back home and land a job as a Nursing assistant at a Mental Rehabilitation Facility. It took a lot of patience, but I remember being extra sensitive toward the patients. Some were there and NEVER had anyone come visit them. This position was too emotionally draining and too slow for me.

One of SAM'S Nephews....

On December 15, 1999 I got on a plane and headed to San Antonio, Texas. I had joined Uncle Sam's military. After taking the ASVAB (Military Test) my scores ranked in the top 97th percentile and I was told that I can pick WHATEVER job I wanted. I signed the dotted line to become a United States Airman! But what job should I pick? I could choose ANY. Had I already had a passion for a particular field the answer to that question would be easy.

Thinking back, I'm shaking my head because I know for a fact that I did absolutely NO research on the field that I chose. The job I chose begins with a B and I know the THICK list of jobs were in alphabetical order, so I probably just picked the FIRST coolest looking one that I came across. I could choose ANY job out the list, and I chose Biomedical Equipment Technician.

Biomedical Equipment Technician is a job that requires you to be able to fix machines in hospitals. When I signed up for the position, the schooling was described as 33 weeks at Lackland Air Force base. This schooling was to be done after the 6-week Basic Military Training which was conducted at that same base. Lackland.

I received my military orders a couple days prior to finishing the 6-week Basic Training. The orders that I received were NOT the same orders in the description for the position I signed my name up for though.

The orders were for my schooling to be 64 weeks long, almost double what I signed up for and at a completely different base.

Half-way into my training I separated from the Air Force with a General Under Honorable Conditions discharge. I'm not going to go into the details of my military experience here, that is a completely different book entirely. I will say it was one of the Best Times of my life though. Fate had me choose the job I did. The Medical Dorm for the Air Force was LIT!

And in my best Forrest Gump voice "that's all I have to say about that"…..

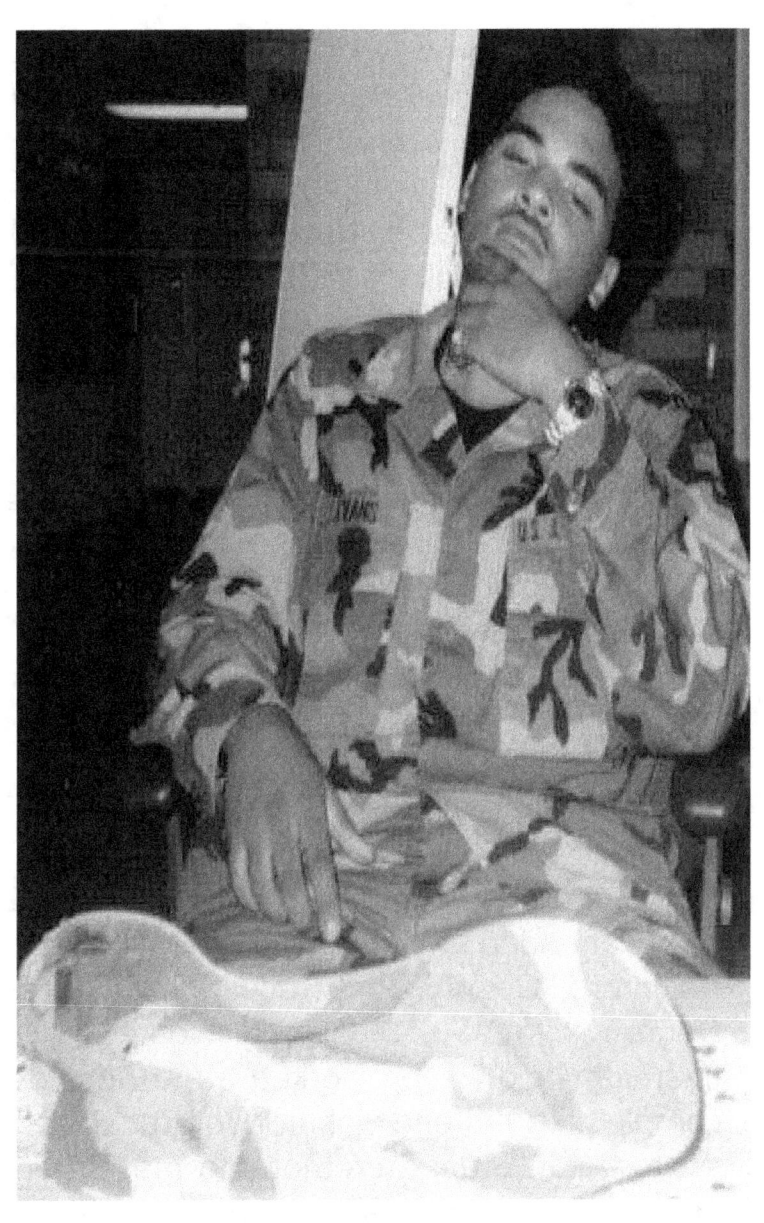

I came back home AGAIN! I left home my Junior year in High School to go to school in Virginia. Graduated high school and left home again to attend Marshall University in the state of West Virginia then came back home. Served The United States Military in the Air Force in Texas, and then came back home.

Six months in the Military, and one of my best friends back home was murdered. I was not able to come home for the funeral. I had just talked to him a week before his death. 6 months after I got back home from the military my other best friend was also gunned down in the streets of Baltimore. The years 2000 and 2001 were life changing.

I worked a couple jobs in my early 20's. I also attended The Community Colleges of Baltimore County and received an Associate Degree with a 3.75 GPA. I worked at Target overnight and I even worked at McDonalds. Just complete dead-end jobs. Well at least what seemed to be dead end jobs to me. When I say dead end, I mean there was no rapid growth and promotion opportunities. Once again, slow moving jobs.

Like Riding a Bike....

Not having a job is one of the worse feelings in the world. I have worked at McDonalds, Target, a Newspaper stand at the Airport, the military, Home Depot, several telemarketing positions, sheet metal fabricator, Used Car Salesman, Nursing assistant and there might be a couple I am leaving out. Working at a dead end feels pretty bad too.

I had to find something where the environment changed frequently. I hate feeling like I am stuck in a bubble. Early on I felt like I knew my worth and hated to settle for less.

One day searching on Craigslist, I ran across a job listing that said, "Part-time work, Full-Time Pay". I click the ad and the ad was very vague. It didn't have much detail other than Customer Service. The ad really harped on the pay. $700+ a week for Part time work sounded GREAT!

I scheduled an interview for a position I knew very little about. Of course, the ad said the work was very easy, and you can make easy money. Still I had no clue as to what I would actually be doing. I went to the interview anyway.

This was the first time I had ever been to a "group" interview before. I came into the office, the secretary asked my name, looked over a sheet and told me to go down the hall first door on the right. I opened the door, and it was a midsized room filled with about 20 chairs with 7 of them already occupied. I got to the back row and find a seat.

When the word interview comes to mind, this setting is not what you typically think of. I was thinking more of a one on one meeting in an office, you know, with a desk.

I got there 10 minutes early and patiently waited as more seats filled up. One lady decided to break the silence in the room and ask if anyone knew what the job was. I remember scanning the room and seeing everyone's face filled with puzzlement as 2 or 3 people responded back, NOPE.

At 11 a.m. sharp, the door to the room opens and two men walk in. There was a black guy and an Eastern Indian man, both dressed in sharp suits. The black gentleman walked to the front of the room toward the dry erase board and the other guy walked to the back of the room and kind of leaned or sat on the radiator directly behind my chair.

I remember the black guy starting the presentation off loud and filled with energy. I would not find out until later that this was his very first Interview Group. He was calm, all smiles and filled with BLING! Earrings, chain, watch and rings. I peeped it all. He didn't have a tie on either. He was fresh!

He conducted the presentation and come to find out it, it was a door to door job. The moment he let the cat out the bag in reference to what the job actually was, I remember seeing about 3 people get up and walk out the room. The man conducting the interview didn't freeze an inch. He didn't ask where they were going, he didn't try and convince them to stay, he just kept it moving.

When I heard door to door, I immediately got excited. This was something that I already had experience with. Just tell me what to say, and if it works for you then it will work for me. I learned that attitude doing Telemarketing.

Everybody is saying the same script, yet some people have more success than others. I excelled at the telemarketing job because of that mindset.

At the end of the group interview, the guy conducting the meeting gave everyone a piece of paper with the script typed on it. It had 3 parts to it. The intro, the body and the close. He read the script through its entirety and asked the group if it seemed pretty simple. Almost in unison, everyone in the group agreed that the script was easy.

He then challenged the group. This interview took place on a Friday, and he challenged everyone, that whoever could memorize the "Intro" of the script, would receive a $50 cash bonus on the spot, on Monday.

The group got excited and I remember the guy behind me leaning up from off the radiator and looking at his watch. He was dressed pretty sharp as well, but less bling bling.

The 2 guys in charge made eye contact and the meeting was concluded. Everyone seemed to all disperse at once without any type of communication among one another. The guy in the back of the room walked to the front of the room and stood near the instructor as he erased the dry erase board.

I left out the room last and left them 2 standing in the room conversing with one another as the door closed. I slowly closed the door because it would have slammed loudly had I not. With one last glimpse inside the room before the door shuts, the black guy makes eye contact with me and nods his head.

Monday comes and I know the intro down pat. To my surprise, out of the 12-remaining people from the interview, only 7 showed back up including myself. Then like clockwork at 11 a.m. The same 2 gentlemen come waltzing into the room, once again looking sharp as a shark's tooth.

They take the same spots in the room as they did on Friday. The black guy, in the front of the room, opens with lots of excitement and energy. "GOOD MORNING everyone" he exclaimed. Then in unison all 7 of us responded back good morning as if it was the worse morning ever.

"No no no!...I SAID GOOD MORNING EVERYONE" he repeats, this time cupping his ear toward the small group. This time we responded back like an erupting volcano!

"That's more like it!" he says, and then follows up with some of the most important words I have ever heard. "It takes Energy to Sell Energy!"

Yes! Energy! We were selling energy. If anyone remembers that 70% rate increase for Baltimore Gas and Electric back in 2007ish then I'm sure you remember people knocking on your doors for the first time trying to sell energy. I'm sure here in 2020, if you live in one of the Energy

Deregulated States, you still have people knocking on your door today!

So, the black guy claps his hands together and with a big smile asks "So, who has the intro memorized? Who wants this $50 today?". He reaches into his back pocket, pulls out his wallet, shuffles through it and pulls out a crisp 50-dollar bill.

He slaps it on the podium and looks around at everyone. A dead silence filled the room as everyone looked around at each other seeing who was going to be the brave soul and go first.

I look around and before he could repeat the question, I raise my hand. I was already confident on knowing the intro of the script verbatim, what I wasn't sure about was speaking in front of everyone.

It was only 9 people, but immediately after he told me to stand up, I felt the butterflies kick in and my palms starting to sweat.

Public Speaking was the only college course that I received a grade less than a B. I passed that class with a C. I got a C not because my material wasn't thorough, but because I stuttered and presented with a very weak nature.

I studied the intro all weekend but forgot to consider that I would have to do it in front of everyone. In the split second of me standing up I thought about that Public Speaking class. I had to dig deeper.

I had to think back to my QB days. I remember thinking about being in a huddle. All I was about to do is call the play! I briefly closed my eyes and took a deep breath then opened my eyes and fixed them on the instructor.

I visualized him being at the door and recite the introduction of the script to a tee. I recited with all the needed punctuations needed and with pauses in the right place and all. There was a WOW factor that came over the room. Another dead silence. Then the guy in the back of the room, leans up from the radiator and starts clapping his hands.

"That was incredible!" he says with his Indian accent. "Wow. Everyone give it up for?" he says and points to me to interject with my name.

"Maurice" I say, like a boss. "Yes Maurice, everyone give it up for Maurice!" he says and starts clapping and walking over to the podium. The room erupts with claps, he grabs the 50-dollar bill and brings it to me. "And HERE, this is for you as promised. Is there anyone else?!" he says full of pride and energy. No one else stood up.

The 2 men went back to their positions in the room and the training started. He basically went over the same exact stuff that he went over on Friday

After going over everything again, he had us break into pairs. Everyone was kind of sitting close to one another and immediately paired up. I was slow to choose and wound up being the only one left without a partner.

After seeing that I had no partner, the guy in the back of the room calls my name and tells me to come to the back of the room where he is standing and that he will be my partner.

The next part of the training is something that I will never forget. In conjunction with the notion that "it takes Energy to sell Energy", this part of the training was geared toward creating energy.

They had us reading the scripts out loud to our partners, and then our partners would read it back. We were to do this about 5 times each, and this was just to get us comfortable with saying it.

Once everyone did it 5 times each, the instructor then got all our attention and said that he now wanted us to "create energy" with our body. Body language.

It was not just shaking your head and flapping your hands around a bit. The body language taught was precise movements at precise times in the script.

It was interesting to learn the moves and I was anxious to give them a try at people's front doors. He told us that everything we come to the people's door with is a prop. So our badge, clipboard and pen were all props and we were to use them as such.

That Monday was set aside for us to train there in the office. For about an hour we rotated partners and did the script with the added body language. Every person I worked with complemented me on my pitch when I finished it.

It was a great feeling, one similar to the feeling I felt playing QB in football. I left the office that day feeling more inspired than when I came. I was motivated to go out and make it happen!

The next day they had us come in at 2 p.m. This time arriving at the room where the training was held, there were about 20 people in the room all wearing blue collard polo type shirts with the Company name on it. They were all full of energy and excitement. It seemed like they were in there practicing.

I spotted 3 of the people from my training class as they stuck out like a sore thumb because they, like myself, didn't have a blue shirt on, and they were all huddled together off to the side of the room.

I walk over to them and join their little congregating. We all just stood off to the side together and watched everyone so animated and full of energy practice their pitch.

There were a lot of laughs going on among the veteran blue shirt wearers, but it was all non-stop communication. I remember paying close attention to how everyone's body language was different. They were all doing basically the same moves, but everyone gave their own energy.

Some looked like robots, very stiff with the combination of moves, while others were extra smooth with their body language. I kept close attention to the ones who looked natural when moving and talking. It wasn't a lot of movement; just certain head gestures and specific hand moves that were done at specific parts of the script.

The first movement was during the intro. When introducing yourself, they wanted us to raise our badge, straight out, at a 90-degree angle with our picture facing the customer and then drop it onto our chest. Not lay it back onto our chest but release it so that it will swing back onto our chest and bounce a little, thus creating energy.

As soon as I drop the badge, I was to swing my pen around like a lasso a little bit in front and to the side of my eye. This movement not only creates energy but draws their eye in close proximity to your eye. I let them know I was just doing some follow-ups in the area as I twirled the pen.

Next I would raise my clip board, and go to the second sheet of paper with nothing but address numbers, and point to their address(that I had already written on the paper prior to knocking) and ask if they were the person in charge of the address.

So for instance, I would look at the address on the second sheet of paper and ask "are you the person in charge of 123 Chief Street?" and I would nod my head yes while I'm asking the question.

If they answered yes, then they were qualified for me to continue to talk to them.

So if they are the person in charge, next I would do the pen twirl again and say "well I'm only doing follow ups in the neighborhood" then I would flip my clipboard over and point to an Energy Deregulation article taped to the back of it and say "because the Government has changed the laws for everyone , you're able to get a discount on your BGE bill".

When I said BGE bill I flipped the clipboard back over and pointed to the top BGE bill of a stack of 10 BGE bills that I had on the clipboard.

While still pointing to the BGE bill, I would then say "see BGE makes their money from delivery and service charges, not the cost of electricity" and shake my head "no" when saying not the cost.

Then I was to raise my eyebrows in excitement and say, "but thanks to the Government, you're now allowed price protection, against rate increases, for free".

When I said price protection, I was to grip my pen as if I was playing rock paper scissors, and I picked rock. When I said rate increases, I stuck my thumb straight up and raised it, and when I said "for free" I open my hand like I picked paper, and glide my hand across the air from left to right like I was wiping something off a table.

The last part was the part that has tickled me for years. It still brings a smile to my face today when I think about it. This last part was the most crucial part of the whole pitch.

It was energy built up(created) in parts of the script that came before. You had to muster up the courage to tell someone to go get their bill. A complete stranger, that was more times than not older than me.

The way they had us do it was by not asking. That is what made it so funny to me. I'm going to TELL a stranger to go get their personal bill, and hand it to me. Not only hand it to me but let me take it with me.

So when it came time to get the bill I had to say "so just like the rest of your neighbors" as I waved the stack of 10 BGE bills in their face then placed them back on the clipboard. "Go get your bill so I can see if your qualified".

When I said go get your bill, I had to take my pen and point into their house over their shoulder, then turn my back to them and act like I was writing something right after saying qualified.

To me that seemed rude, but in sales it was called taking control. I wasn't sure if that part would work, but I was eager to find out.

Because I knew the gestures down pat, I kept my eyes fixated on the guy who seemed to be doing all the motions effortlessly as the veterans practiced.

When it came time to ask for the BGE bill, he was demanding and when he turned his back, he was smooth. He dressed differently than everyone else too.

While mostly everyone in the room had on khaki pants or shorts, there were a couple of jean wearers. The one guy who stood out though had on dress pants and dress shoes.

He had a crisp crease in his pants and his blue shirt was tucked in tightly. He had what appeared to be diamonds in both ears, a watch, a bracelet and necklace with a pendant. Not only was he the best dressed representative and did the script better than everyone else, he was also the loudest in the room.

In sports, there is always one common denominator. "If you want to BE THE BEST, you have to BEAT THE BEST". He was clearly the best in the room as far as practice was concerned. If this opportunity was making him good money, then I wanted to mimic and then surpass him.

Soon, the 2 bosses entered the room and the room got quiet. The quietness only lasted for a split second as the black boss erases the dry erase board then turns and yells, "Who's House?" and then the group responded back in unison "BLUE'S HOUSE!". The chant went on 2 more times and then the entire room started clapping, not in unison, more like a pep rally.

Then the boss went into another chant.

"Who's ready to make some money?" and the crew responded, "I AM!" This chant was done 3 times as well.

The energy in the room was amazing. The way the boss commanded the room reminded me of my football days. He was the coach. He got everyone amped. He gave us the game plan for the day.

Today, which was my first official day to go out and observe someone and maybe knock, the boss stressed the importance of rebuttals.

Rebuttals are persuasive comebacks to any objection that a customer may give you. He said that it was important because not everyone makes a decision, off of your first try. He said you should never leave a door without giving at least 3 rebuttals. He said if they are not convinced by then, they will probably close the door in your face anyways.

He broke the entire group into 4 groups and each of the new people, myself included, were in different groups. He then assigned each group an area on this jumbo-sized map of Baltimore county that was taped to the dry erase board.

Each group's area was highlighted in a different color, and then each group was handed sheets of paper with only their area on the page.

My group's color was green. The area we were working was one that I was already pretty familiar with. It was not too far from where I grew up so I was already comfortable. A middle working-class neighborhood, with mostly homeowners, not renters.

The group that I was assigned to was not the same group the guy with the dress slacks was in. I remember wondering how many deals he was going to do that day. Then I started to look around at the people in my green group and wondered who will be training me today. Then all sorts of negative thoughts started forming like; I hope they make a lot of sales, I hope they are easy to get along with, I hope I can keep up.

That's when the boss comes over to my group with a blue collared shirt in his hand and hands it to me. He then told me who I would be working with. A young lady maybe slightly older than myself who had been with the company for a little over 3 months. I definitely noticed her when I first came in but was more focused on dude with the slacks.

How could I not notice her? She was the only one in there with a khaki skirt on. Thick thighs, thick calf's, fresh all white low top NIKE Air Force Ones. She was light skin with long pressed jet-black hair pass her shoulders. Her lip gloss was popping, and she wore hoop earrings. Her skirt came a few inches above the knee, but the tight fit could not hide the wagon she was dragging, if you know what I mean. LOL

She was FINE! PERIODT!

And she smelled amazing.

I could tell that she wasn't from Baltimore from the moment she spoke. Baltimore has a very distinct accent. I didn't know where she was from, but I knew I'd find out. The one thing I also noticed, right away, was that she didn't have a wedding ring on. No imprint on the finger or anything.

The boss introduced us, and we got slightly acquainted. Well her only question for me was, "have you ever done this before?". I told her I use to knock doors to shovel snow, should be like riding a bike. She said as long as you are good with people, you should do well.

The boss then announces that he is giving out the keys to the drivers. Apparently, the company had 4 vans, at least. Each crew got their key, and my group was last. I didn't know who he was going to hand the key to, but I was curious to find out after the guy with dress pants got the key to their group. To my surprise, he gave the key to my trainer. So she must be a team leader.

The Boss drew a picture of the pay structure and promotion bonuses during the interview and training day. He was a Manager, the young lady was a Team Leader, and I was just a team member. So she got paid a little extra for every deal that anybody on her team made.

The manager got paid on every deal done by the 4 teams.

Right after the manager handed my leader the keys, the room door flung open and in came this short white guy. He was chubby with a short blonde haircut with shades pushed back on his head.

I remember him wearing distressed jeans with a white V-neck t-shirt and cowboy boots. His little stubby arms were full of hair. He had a watch on and a blinged out ring on his ring finger. He was grasping a large 7-11 Slurpee cup.

He took a sip, lets out an "AHhhhh..." then yells out "WHO'S HOUSE?" and of course the room erupts together and says "BLUE'S HOUSE".

He then says he spots some new faces in the group. He excitedly stated that if we were here on Tuesday, that meant we made it through the interview and indoor training from Friday and Monday. He assured us new people that today was only an observation day.

He then introduces himself as the Boss of the company. I remember thinking how he was the least best dressed in the room, including the reps in their blue collared shirts. I'm sure they were no ordinary jeans, and even the T-shirt was probably designer. It just wasn't what I expected the REAL Boss to wear.

He gives the group a pep talk and then adjourns the meeting. Everyone started to head for the exit. You could feel the energy as the room grew loud like a High School cafeteria that just dismissed lunch.

As my leader was gathering her things, I scanned the room and saw the other 3 new people engaged in conversation with their leader. The guy with the dress pants on was still animated, even when talking to his new rep. My leader on the other hand seemed, not robotic but not as full of energy as the other guy.

She zipped up a book bag and then proceeds to ask if I could carry it for her. Before I even pick it up I think to myself that I hope she doesn't think I'm going to be her little slave, but being the gentleman that I can be, I immediately picked it up and said "no problem".

We head out of the office into the parking lot and all you see is a swarm of blue shirts. Everyone is congregating near their team van or headed toward it. I follow my team leader and remember telling myself how I had to keep my composure and be professional. At that moment I re-realized how fine she was.

We get to our van and she instructs me to sit in the front. She tells me that, that will be my seat until we get someone new. The van was a white 8 passenger minivan and from the looks of things our crew was 4 deep. A girl and a guy huddled at our van, and were there laughing and carrying on as we approached. My team leader introduced me to them and I could instantly tell that they were a tad bit younger. Early 20's maybe late teens.

My leader hits the remote unlock button and then one of the guys swings back the sliding door. I hop in the front as instructed, they hop in the back and the leader hops in the driver's seat. I place the bookbag between my legs and she pops open the glasses' storage area on the ceiling of the van.

When it opens out falls a blue string. She tugs on the string and out pops an ID badge connected to it. She gives it to me and tells me it is a temporary badge for the day. I look at it and to my dismay it was some African man's ID. I stare at the badge with a look of bewilderment on my face then I look up at her.

She laughs as we make eye contact and before I could say anything, she says "don't worry, nobody ever looks at our badges". I stare back down at the badge and try and pronounce the guys name in my head. I don't think I had any luck.

We pull out the parking lot and head toward our destination. It was a beautiful spring day in Baltimore, nothing but sunshine and hi 70 degree weather. I had on a pair of khaki pants and a fresh pair of all white high top Nike Air Force 1's. My fresh white polo was straight out the packaging. It wasn't a Ralph Lauren Polo, some no name brand, but it was fresh and clean. I had to change to the Blue one. I had an all-white fitted hat that sat on top of my head that had two braids in my hair.

Along the way, she pulls out a stack of BGE bills and hands them back to one of the other reps. She instructs them to take a few and pass them back up. She reaches on the side of her chair, grabs a clip board, then hands it to me along with 2 out of the remaining BGE bills. "Here you go. Remember, this is just a prop." She says and then turns the music up.

I remember it being a smooth comfortable ride. We got to our destination in no time and like I said I was already a bit familiar with the area.

She parked at the end of the street and pulled out the xerox copies of the maps. She had three of them and scanned them all until she found the one for the exact spot we were at. She puts that map on top and looks back to the other reps.

"So, which one of you guys want this area?" she says holding the map up between her fingers. Almost immediately the guy says, "I got it!" and grabs the map. He places the map underneath everything that was on his clipboard gives one good tug on his cap while looking in the rear-view mirror and then blurts out "Hit Your Goals!" and the 2 remaining ladies in the van respond back in unison "Hit YOUR GOAL!".

He swings the van door open, hops out, sets his clipboard on the seat and adjust his clothes. He then grabs the clipboard and swings the door shut. He put his pen in his mouth and then lifted all the papers up to look at his map. We pulled off while he was still looking at his map.

With one of the other maps in her lap, the team leader drives to the next drop off spot. Not too far from the first dropoff, we park again. This time she hands the map to the young lady and proceeds to give her instructions.

"Ok now, make sure you work the entire map. Draw a line on the map with your pen as you work the street. If you get done them all before 6pm go straight back to where you started, if not, wait until 6pm to restart from the beginning of your map. Remember, breathe and smile. Don't be stiff be extra fluid. It takes energy to sell energy. If you have any problems call me".

The young lady looks at her map and nods her head. She swings open the other door of the van and as she exits, she shouts out "Hit Your Goals!". The leader responded, "hit your goal" and I also, with a second delay, responded "hit your goal". She closes the door and without hesitation she headed toward her first door. Before she reached the steps to the front porch, we pulled off again.

With the remaining map on her lap, the team leader takes us to our area. Once again not too far from the last drop off. She parks the van and then looks at the map for a few seconds.

After coming up with her game plan she pulls the keys out of the ignition and says "alright, so you are my trainee for the day. That is how I will address you when I introduce you. I don't want you to say ANYTHING. When I introduce you, just nod your head. If at any time the customer asks you a question, tell them they can ask me or get my attention. But at no time do I want you to speak. Got it?"

With a little grin on my face I say, "got it". Noticing the grin on my face, she then responds and says "You'd be surprised at how many times I've had a trainee speak AFTER I told them the exact same thing. It can kill the deal, and that's my money". The seriousness sank in and I erased the smirk off my face, bit my bottom lip and nodded my head.

She then goes on to get out the van. When she opened her door to get out, I did the same. She locks the door and then heads around to my side. With her clipboard in hand, she raises the pile of BGE bills (at least 7) and writes the name of the street on a paper called a walk sheet, which is designed to keep record of your contacts.

She instructs me to do the same and then tells me to write everything that she writes on her sheet, on my sheet.

I instantly feel butterflies as we both walk up to the first house. We get to the porch and she positions me behind her a couple of steps before she rings the doorbell. She pushes the doorbell and turns and looks at me and says with her eyes wide as apples, "Remember, don't say anything!".

She held the screen door open with her knee and waited. She took a quick glimpse back at me at told me to look busy. All I did was look as if I was reading something off my clipboard. 2 Seconds after she turned back around the main door opens.

A young white lady maybe in her mid-40's opens the door. Startled, as she looks my leader in the eyes and then myself, she says "excuse me, please release my door". She grabs hold of the screen door handle and pulls the door shut.

"Now may I help you?" the young lady asked with conviction.

She had her hair up in a ponytail and was wearing a pink and black Nike sports bra and all pink leggings to match. You could tell she had already been working out from the darker pink spots on her bra that was left from perspiration. She had a big diamond ring on and a tattoo on the front of her right shoulder.

My leader takes a step back and crosses her arms down in front of her waist. Without any hesitation she went into the most melodic pitch I had ever heard. It was like she was singing. She was serenading the customer. She was serenading me to the point that before I knew it the deal was done and she was telling me to come on to the next door.

She was a PRO! I was thankful that I was placed on her team. The only problem was that she was also very physically attractive. The more

I realized how gorgeous she was, the more I realized she wasn't paying me any mind. She was focused. She was on a mission.

6pm came and we finally took a break. We went to the van and sat in it. At this point I was anxious to start knocking on my own. She had closed 8 people, which amounted to 16 deals. 1 deal for gas and 1 deal for electric for each customer. At $25 dollars a deal she had already made in a couple hours, what some were making for a week's worth of work.

$25 X 16 deals is $400. Back then $10 an hour was minimum wage. 40 hours working at McDonalds was the equivalent to what she had done in 4 hours. This was a no-brainer for me!

My deals at the rep Level were worth $15 a piece, $30 per person if they used both gas and electric. Signing up 3 people a day was worth more in a week than working a week at McDonalds.

I had my head stuck on closing 8 people every day just like she had just done. $2000 a week and more in a week than McDonalds makes in a month ($1600) was mind boggling.

This is not to mention the overrides she receives from the reps. $10 for every deal we make. So if the other 2 reps made 16 sales a piece as well, then the leader was sitting on $720 FOR THE DAY!

That is the type of numbers I was pushing into my calculator on my cellphone. $720 a day times 5 days is $3,600. At McDonalds it would be $3,200 in TWO MONTHS!

Just when I was about to calculate how much that is for a year she interrupted my train of thought by saying "so, what you think so far? Do you think it is something you can do? Pretty simple right?".

I see her shuffle her stack of filled out contracts to get them all in sync and then lock eyes with her and say "most definitely! I'm trying to knock today!".

She grins. It was the first time that she gave me a genuine expression of warmth. She clips her contracts underneath her street sheet and stack of about 15 BGE bills on her clipboard.

"You sure now?" she says with a sarcastic tone. "Cause I can keep knocking and you can keep watching if you want. It's your time and it's your money" she added on.

"No, I'm ready. You made it look pretty simple. I think I got this!" I counter respond quite confidently.

"Ok let me see how they are doing and then I'm a let you practice with me" she replies.

She pulls out her cell phone calls one of the reps. Initially I thought the female rep was having a good day by the way the leader displayed excitement during the conversation.

It wasn't until the end of the conversation that my thoughts swayed into the opposite direction. Once I heard her end the call by saying "Alright, just focus on 2. We have 2 more hours, just get at least 2 more and finish the day with 4" I knew her day was nowhere near the type of day the leader was having.

She then calls the male rep. The conversation went the exact same as the conversation with the other rep. The only difference, she instructed him to get 2 more and finish the day with 5.

A little unclear, after she hangs up with the male rep, I immediately ask how many deals have they done. Already knowing that the leader was up to 16 deals, I wasn't sure if she was telling them to get 2 more deals, or 2 more people which would equal 4 more deals.

She clarifies that the female rep had 2 dual fuels which meant 2 people who had both gas and electric, and the guy had 3 dual fuels.

So the leader had more duel fuels,8, than the two reps combined. Still she had made more money from their work ($100) than a McDonalds employee made with their own 8 hours($80).

I then ask how long have they been doing this and she lets me know that the guy had been around for almost a month, and that this was the girls first full week of work. Meaning she was right where I was at now, a week prior, a first day rep.

I then ask her; how long has she been knocking doors. We lock eyes again, and once again she has a grin on her face. This time the grin was more of an accomplishment look, rather than the sarcastic grin from before. She knew that I was asking because she had way more deals done.

"A little over 2 months. But trust and believe that I started out just like her. The key is to show up every day and just be consistent. I know the script like my favorite song and I just dance with it using my body language" she said as her grin turned into a full fledge smile.

It made me think back to the first deal she made with the white lady. I remember thinking that when the white lady first abruptly closed her screen door, it was going to be a definite NO, but the melodic sounds that came out of my leader's mouth was astounding and mesmerizing and she closed the deal.

I remember thinking that I would be doing 8 people a day in no time. If there was one thing I could do, is mimic success. I always had the mentality that if it works for you, it will work for me too and little did I know, I would be absolutely correct.

I hit the streets running that day. I closed my first deal that night and never looked back. For the next year or so I would make more money in that industry than everything else combined that came before.

I sat with millionaires on a monthly basis. I trained 100's of reps and enrolled 1000's of customers. There was NOTHING like it. Or so I thought.

Amid my success in the energy industry, my life took a drastic turn. Not a turn for the worse, but just in a total different direction.

THE INTERNET

By the time I hit my mid to late 20's, most of my peers that I had grown up with had already had their first child and many were on to their second and third. I was just having my first child. A little girl.

The circumstances surrounding the birth of my daughter along with a few other underlying factors, forced me to take up the roll of being home to help take care of my daughter. This meant no more knocking doors. At least for now.

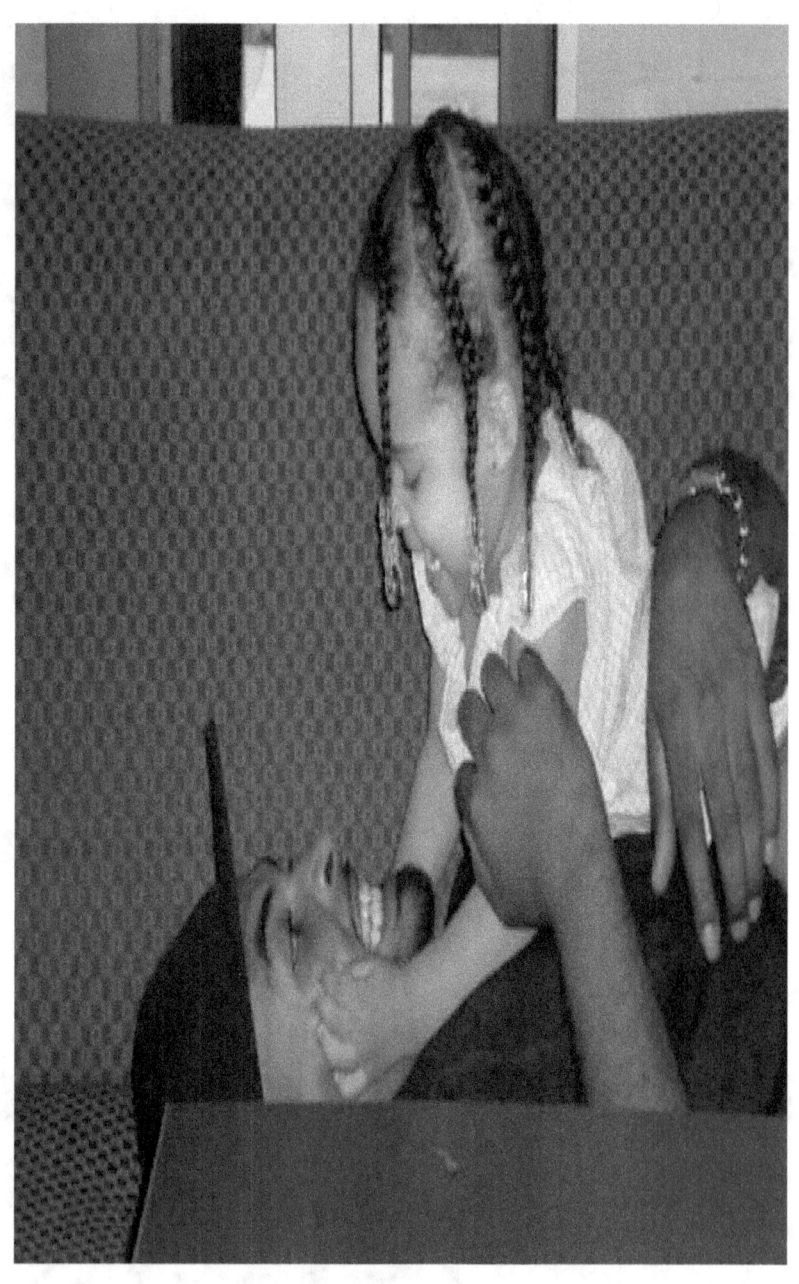

    I had to find a way to make money from home. The internet had a plethora of opportunities at my disposal, but the last thing I wanted to do was invest money into some get rich quick scheme and get scammed. I didn't even want to have to invest any money at all if possible.

I pulled up good old Craigslist once again. I refined my search to "work from home positions" and went scrolling through the post to see which one seemed most enticing. So many to choose from, hell all of them looked enticing. All promising big returns for little effort.

Then I came to this one post. It had all the same claims as the previous opportunities, yet this one had a very long description. The description actually detailed, what the opportunity consisted of. It gave a breakdown of what you would do day to day. It seemed sketchy, but then again all of the work from home opportunities seemed sketchy.

After reading the description in its entirety, I knew what I would be getting myself into. This was adult content, and I would be soliciting a website for customers to view Live webcams. It would never be me on the cam, I would just direct people to the site and when they buy, I get paid. If there was one thing I know I remember hearing time and time again in the sales world is that SEX SELLS!

This was back when Yahoo still had chatrooms. The crazy part about it, is that I was already familiar with the sales experience from the customer side.

I had already been in Yahoo chatrooms in the past and found myself unexpectedly ending up on some random sex website after I clicked a link in the room.

The task was pretty simple. I make a yahoo account with a female's name and picture. I had to make sure the profile picture was something sexy and her name had to be something enticing. They already had a website to choose pictures from of webcam models that worked with the site.

Create a profile page with a link directed to the webcam site that was unique to my "affiliate" account. This was the first time I heard the term affiliate.

There was a link provided for me that was linked directly to my information to be paid. The link was to be put in the profile so that when guys went to it and clicked it, it redirected them to an unsuspecting website which where they can then decide if they want to watch Live videos of girls.

(THE ORIGINAL ONLY FANS)

Yahoo Chatroom

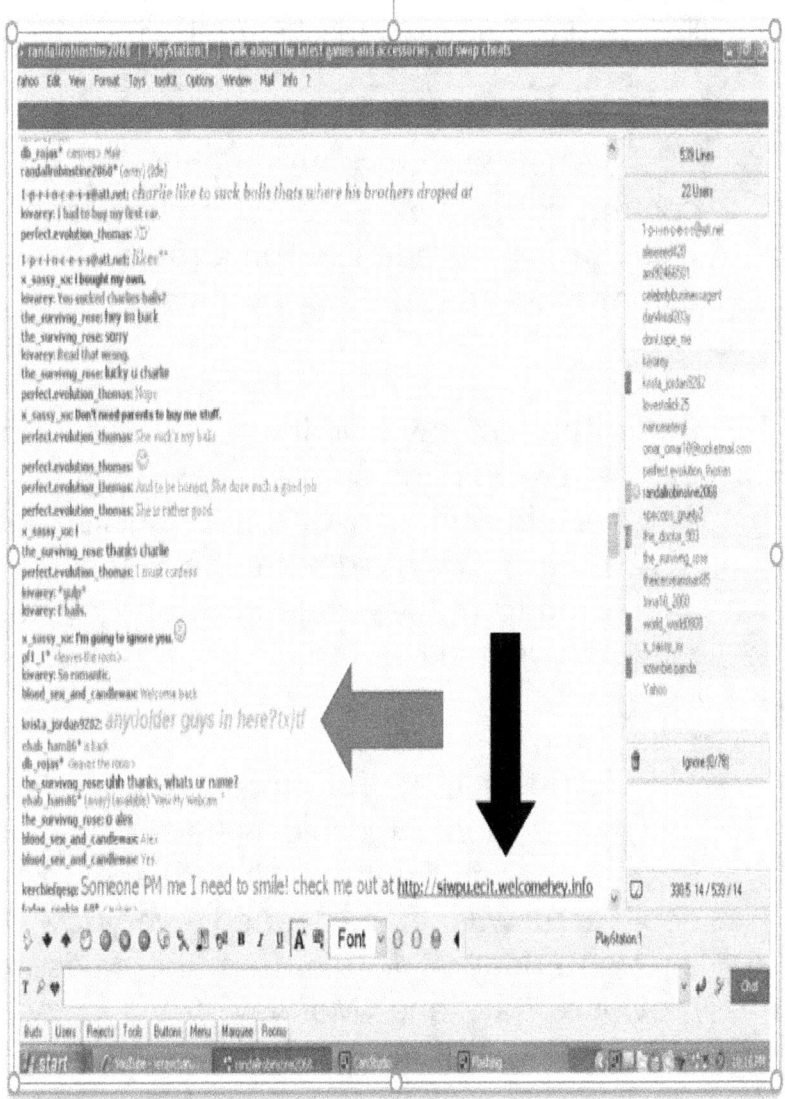

All I had to do was go into every chatroom and paste the sentence "see me LIVE in my profile" and sure enough people would go and click the link. If someone clicked the link they were taken to a page where they could spend $25 and get $50 worth of cam time.

When the customer spends the $25 I was commissioned $50. 200% Commission! That is what struck my attention on Craigslist, the 200% commission described in the details.

The first day I did it was a Friday. I followed the instructions and sure enough, I made 2 sales. Another enticing part of the Craigslist post was DAILY PAY! They told me to send them an email after I made my first sale so that they could set me up to get paid.

When I sent the email, they replied that I had two options. I could instantly be paid with PayPal or I could get a debit card sent to me. The debit card was to be loaded everyday Monday through Friday at 10 a.m from the sales from the previous day and Monday from sales made Friday through Sunday.

At the time I had a PayPal account, but I didn't have a PayPal debit card. Since I didn't really use PayPal that often yet, I elected to get the prepaid debit card. Also, if I elected to get paid via PayPal, the pay was every week on Wednesdays instead of daily.

I was told that they would be mailing it out through FedEx express and that I should look forward to receiving the debit card no later than Monday. They told me to keep working and that I would be paid on Monday from all the weekend sales. This enticed me to continue to work this new opportunity through the weekend.

The shutoff time for the day was midnight. All sales made by midnight would be paid the following pay day. This had me up until midnight on my first weekend doing this. I was up anyway watching Sunday Night Football as my Baltimore Ravens beat the New York Jets.

I made 2 sales on Friday, 3 sales on Saturday but only 1 on Sunday. I stayed in front the computer ALL DAY, watching Football on my TV and copying and pasting "**Free Cam Shows**

in my profile" in as many Yahoo chat rooms as I could.

Yahoo had the best chatrooms. To me, Yahoo chat rooms were my childhood Facebook. With 1000's of room to choose from, you could always find a chat with someone. With this opportunity, I focused on the "U.S. States" chatrooms. Each state would have up to 10 chatrooms. So that was roughly 500 rooms to bounce around.

If you ever saw the name "MsMakeYouCum" on Yahoo chat, that was the profile I was using.

After midnight on that first Sunday I remember deciding not to get back online until my debit card came in the mail. I didn't want to continue spending my time until I knew it was real. The website had a tracking system that would let you know how many people clicked your link and how many of those actually spent the $25.

Soon as midnight hits, the statistics clear back to zero. Opening up the webpage and seeing zero, I didn't find myself being as enthused as when I saw the accumulated $300 up until 11:59pm.

Monday morning comes and I am anxious. I know I put in at least 20 hours on the computer and I was ready to collect. I turn on my computer and open up the website. I look at the statistics page and it still reflects all zeros.

The reason I was checking was because on Saturday, one of the sales I made that day came when I was not even online. I made a sale early in the morning and then when I logged on later that evening the statistics showed 2 sales, before I made the third one.

While waiting patiently for my card to arrive, I could not help but work some more. Instead of going to the yahoo chatrooms, I decided to make 5 more profiles. I figured the more models the more chances for sales.

MsJuicyBooty- a white model

MsPhatAzz- a black model

TastyCakes- a Puerto Rican model

Asian_Sin_sation- an Asian model

Cam_Starz- a variety of models

I think back and laugh. If you ever saw any of these names in a Yahoo chatroom, they were mine. If you ever went to the profile, clicked the link and bought time, LOL THANK YOU!

So now I had 6 profiles to use as my ammunition, if so happens the card comes in the mail.

I will never forget, 10 a.m. came and still no card. When I went to the site, the statistics reflected that I had been paid out the $300. My heart started to race. My breathing changed. When I saw "paid out" I immediately thought I had been scammed.

I click on the "contact us" link on the website and aggressively punch the keys on the keyboard. I quickly type them a message stating that I had not received my card yet, but the website said I had been paid.

Within 10 minutes I got a response. I was surprised because the website stated that they were in Henderson Nevada which meant it was 7 a.m. Nonetheless it was a timely response.

The guy who replied let me know that he was the owner of the company and assured me that I had nothing to worry about. He said he looked up the tracking and my FedEx package was scheduled to be delivered some time that day. I never spoke to him on the phone, just email.

I kid you not, not even 10 minutes after receiving the email, the doorbell rang. I dashed up the stairs from out of the basement and dart to the front door. I open it up and there standing on the porch is a FedEx delivery woman. She had a large FedEx envelope in one hand and a handheld device in the other.

She says that she has a package that needs signing for and my eyes lit up like a kid in GameStop with unlimited purchase potential.

I sign the handheld device and grab the envelope. I thank the young lady and before she could key in whatever she needed to key in her device, my screen door was closed, front door was shut and I was probably half way down the stairs to the basement before she got off my front porch.

I get into the basement and flop down in my computer chair and roll a little bit across the floor. I pull the tab on the envelope and open it up. Inside was a blank white letter-sized envelope. I pull the white envelope out and could feel the weight of the debit card shift as it slid to the other end of the envelope.

The white envelope was sealed so I had to open it as well. When I did, out popped a blue debit card with the company's logo on it. The card also said "Temporary" in the spot where my name would go. A white sticker also on the front of the card gave instructions on how to active it. There were two options, by phone or by internet.

I chose the internet route since the internet was already open on my computer. I followed the instructions to a tee and activated the card. I remember my heart racing and moving extra fast with my typing. Once complete, it told me to expect a new card within 7 to 10 business days.

With my heart still racing, this time racing with excitement and not disappointment, I threw some clothes on to run to an ATM machine. The closest one was at a corner store 3 blocks away.

This was not just 3 ordinary blocks. These were blocks in the crime riddled streets of East Baltimore City. I remember clutching the debit card directly in my hand inside my hoodie front pocket. I held it so tight for those 3 blocks that it made my hand sweaty.

I get to the corner store and the ATM is all the way in the back of the store. It was an extremely tight spot to walk to get to the ATM when trying to get by other people in the store.

I pull the card out, give one good scan around the store to see if anyone is watching me, then swipe the card.

So it was supposed to be $300 on there, but I definitely was not about to draw all of it off at once, although I kind of wanted to. I key in my pin then push the button to dispense 50 bucks.

My heart was probably beating at its fastest rate at this time. Butterflies were starting to build up in my stomach like the ones you get in football for the opening kickoff.

When the screen said "PLEASE TAKE YOUR MONEY AND YOUR RECEIPT" I could have bear hugged that machine and picked it up. In my mind I think I was doing the dance "the whop". I did not want to show emotions in this store though. Especially not at the ATM.

The ATM goes to dispense my funds, and this is something I will never forget, out came 5 blank white pieces of paper the same size as a real bill. My elation goes straight to rage as I think the store or ATM is trying to pull a fast one.

Forgetting about where I was and not wanting to show emotion, I blurt out "WHAT THE FUCK IS THIS?" as I grab the pieces of paper along with my receipt.

I check the ATM screen one last time to make sure the transaction is finished and then head for the line. It was maybe 3 people in line and I walked up behind the third person and let out a louder than normal huff of breath.

After hearing the huff and probably feeling my energy, the lady in front of me turns with a grin and lets me know that I just have to turn the paper in, to the guy at the register. Clearly, she had used this store's ATM in the past.

My nerves calm a little and my breathing went back to silent. I stood in line and waited my turn. It wasn't long before I was in front of the line.

The cashier stood behind a plexiglass wall that sat on top of a long counter at the store's entrance. There was a small opening maybe 12 inches by 12 inches in the plexiglass. Behind the glass is a Pakistani man short in stature.

I didn't say a word. I'm sure he already heard the "what the fuck" that I let out my mouth back at the ATM. I just set the 5 pieces of paper on the counter inside the opening of the plexiglass. The cashier immediately snatched them off the counter and opened the register. I could hear as he counted out five bills twice, once when counting the blank pieces of paper then a second time when counting out 5 ten dollar bills.

He then says, "Here you go buddy" and gives me the cash. I thank him and my rage immediately turned back to joy. I folded the bills a clasped them tight with the debit card all in one hand back inside my hoodie pocket. I had to head back through "the jungle" of those 3 blocks back home.

It wasn't quite a speed-walk, but I'm sure my walk back home was a tad bit faster than a normal pace. It was an all uphill walk back, and because the alley that led to my backyard came before the actual street where the front door was, I decided to turn up the alley.

I passed a few older guys working on a truck and it was 2 or 3 dogs barking from their yards. The last few feet from my house seemed like it was going in slow motion. "This was REAL! ALL THE POSSIBILITIES" I remember thinking to myself.

The backdoor gave immediate entrance to the basement. I go in the house and flop back in my chair again. This time I deliberately rolled toward the computer.

I move the mouse to unlock the screen protector on the monitor and the company website is still on the screen. I click the "contact us" link again and quickly deliver the message that I had received my card. Once I finished the message, I quickly open Yahoo Chatrooms.

It was all a numbers game. The more people who saw your profile page, the more people you had click the link, the more people you had buy. I had to come up with creative ways to drive traffic to the profile pages and finally I found an avenue that skyrocketed my sales.

As time went on, posting in the chatrooms became saturated. Every other person posting was a fake cam model. After a few months of success, the sales stayed the same, but the time I had to put in increased. I had to get back to making $100-$200 a day in 4 hours or less.

So I took my marketing strategies to Craigslist! This is when things really started to pick up. Craigslist had a section designated for "escorts". So every guy who would view my post was already looking to "hook up". All I did was make Craigslist Ads that drove traffic to my yahoo profiles.

Things were running smoothly again, and I didn't have to put in as much time again. I wasn't making a whole lot of money, but it was enough to survive and I had a lot more free time than most.

After almost a year of making my little $800 to $1200 a week, things took a drastic turn. Craigslist started charging for their Escort Ads. Depending on the city, the price was all the way up to $50 for ONE AD! I was posting 20 to 25 Ads

EVERY DAY for FREE to sustain my mediocre success. Craigslist ultimately discontinued the erotic section for various reasons.

A website called Backpage had a little bit of traction but no where near as much as Craigslist. So I found myself spending more time again trying to consistently make the same amount of money.

This is when I knew I had to start looking for something else. Besides, I had a baby girl, so this wasn't something I wanted to make a career out of. Tits and ass on my screen all day making ads and having to hurry and change the screen any time I heard someone coming down the steps.

All the T-N-A on my Computer, I'm sure if someone got hold of that PC, they would have thought the owner was some sicko pervert. I wouldn't say that, I could just stomach the images without letting it entice me.

Now that I knew the online opportunities do pay out, well I was at least more trusting because this one did, I searched the internet again for an opportunity. I figured if I found one opportunity that paid out 200% commission, there had to be another.

So I searched "200% commission" on Craigslist. Sure enough, another opportunity popped up. This time the opportunity had nothing to do with the Adult Entertainment Industry. I was instantly drawn to the ad. I clicked it and read it in its entirety. An actual product that people can use. This was perfect.

This time the opportunity had a residual income aspect to it. The first opportunity opened my eyes to "affiliate marketing" and this opportunity opened my eyes to "residual income". Sometimes things don't click in your mind and in your thoughts until you personally experience them.

The opportunity I now had was a membership opportunity. You paid $40 upfront and then $20 a month there after. Then every time you got someone else to pay $40 you got paid $80. Every time they paid $20 a month, you made $8. There was definitely a catch though that I wouldn't learn until later after joining. It was definitely in the fine print at the time I signed up though.

I'm trying to be as descriptive as possible without naming the actual company. I'm sure anyone reading this though and has done the same opportunity KNOWS EXACTLY what opportunity I am referring to. I have nothing negative to say about the company. They are probably still alive and ticking as we speak.

That one company opened up a lot of people's eyes. A lot of people saw success who had never seen online success before. Every week there were stories upon stories of people SUCCEEDING.

The thing that set them apart from most "work from home opportunities" was clearly the 200% commission and the residual income.

With all of the competition I had to find a way to stand out. So while working that opportunity, I searched the internet through the enormous amount of "free" work from home opportunities. I added 2 more totally different opportunities to the one paid membership opportunity and created one mega opportunity. I had benefits, services and a product all in one.

Then there was an opportunity that took a lot of people by surprise. In my opinion, I think the premise behind the opportunity is what brought it so much success. Without me naming the company, anyone who got involved with it would know which one I am referring to when I say that the premise was for everyone to become an IBO.

Becoming an IBO was an "IDEA" and the "IDEA" was sold. This was the first time I had ever heard the term. It stood for Independent Business Owner. The internet was buzzing and waking people up to internet marketing. People that I had introduced the 200% commission opportunity to and declined were reaching out asking me to join them in this new "make money from home thing".

I had some people jump ship to the new "IDEA" from my opportunity. I definitely kept an eye on them and then after maybe a solid year or 2 they shut their site down. I didn't see it coming at all. I can not remember all the details I just remember seeing it on Facebook and then researching it myself.

I never made it to the level of comfort I wanted to before life came calling. Although my tax records for those years reflect pretty good numbers life called and everything was put on hold.

I moved out of state for a couple years and hit RAGGEDY ROCK BOTTOM. I came back to Baltimore October 2018 on a mission! My goal has been to start from scratch and build something even bigger and better than before!

This time around my mind is stuck on leaving a **LEGACY**!

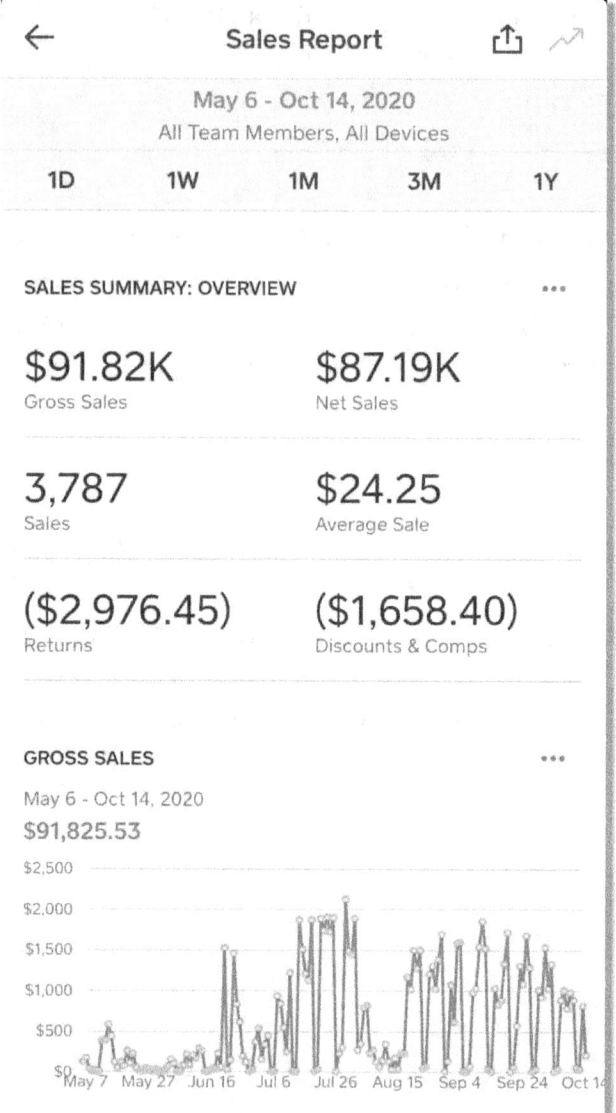

My Rich Friend and Poor Friend

There are so many people that believe life "just ain't right". I mean come on, here you are working hard day and night, week after week, year after year and yet your income does not warrant you enough money to buy you a beer. On the flip side of things, you know people who don't even shed a drop of sweat and yet they live rich without debt. If you truly believe that the Universe has it out for you to lose and you were only born to suffer and struggle, then you are thinking exactly like a poor person stuck in a bubble. But if you believe and KNOW that you are the MASTER ARCHITECHT of your fate and control the helm of the ship we call life, then you are thinking along the SAME lines as ANY RICH Person currently or EVER, and you will be RIGHT!

Understanding the way that millionaires think, is the main ingredient in the formula to wealth. Most wealthy people will tell you that they just played the cards they were dealt. The secret is entangled in the attitude toward wealth and nothing else. Let's approach the psychological aspect of what rich people know about "self".

Now, more than ever before, the gap between the rich and the poor is growing. The rich are becoming richer while the poor are becoming even poorer. This is not just a cliché saying any more. This is supported by factual data. To help us understand the satirical situation, we need to dive into the mentality of the rich and blessed people and compare it with the way the poor and underprivileged people think and perceive life. So much weighs on perception and how one views things to truly be. Here are ten distinct differences I noticed between my Rich Friend and my Poor Friend for you to see. While reading the differences in the two, try to assess your own mindset and see what you want to do.

But remember that by defining 'rich' and 'poor' I am not referring to an individual's current bank account size, but rather, I am referring to the state of mind. A human mind is so powerful it can create both assets and liabilities. If you have a mind conditioned to be poor, no matter what wealth you have today you can lose it all for sure. On the other hand, if you have the mind of a rich person's, you can create your wealth from scratch or get it all back faster than it took you the first time, even if you lose it all today.

> **Rich People Believe They Create their Own Destiny; Poor People Think It's Predestined**
>
> ▸ **Destiny vs Action**
>   Rich people: amazing life creation
>   Poor people: slaves of own destiny
>
> ▸ **Control vs Out-of-Control**
>   Rich people: take full accountability on actions
>   Poor people: lives an unruly life
>
> ▸ **CONCLUSION: if you want to be rich, first be accountable for every action you take!**
>
> ▸

1. My Rich Friend Preaches that They Created their own fate while my Poor Friend is comfortable believing life is already all planned out

Fate refers to the predetermined course of events in one's life. The idea of Fate has a deep history and divine intervention is the most popular belief. People trust that their lives depend on the will of a supernatural being. All of the actions are in vain if it does not coincide with the will of the divine.

✓ **Fate versus Action**

My Rich Friend

My Rich friend has created an amazing life because they did not believe in predetermined fate. Instead, they believe that life is what they make it. If you relax all day and wait for the big fruit to fall into your mouth, nothing will move. Everything will stay in its place unless you make it shake. Like Newton's Law of Motion, "Unless acted upon by a net external force, a body at rest remains at rest and a body in motion remains in motion". This science also true in real life and is how my rich friend approaches. For rich people, they know they are responsible for their own. They create their own fate and not the economy, luck or something else they know.

My Poor Friend

My Poor friend, in the end, believes that they are destined to whatever life sends them. Whatever they do, adversaries come no matter how they try and shake them.

- ✓ **Accounted for versus Unaccounted for**

My Poor Friend

My Poor friend believes an unruly life is cool. Their existence is very unpredictable never know what they might do. When they act, the conclusion is usually over the top. Then they point the finger at everyone else other than themselves when they flop.

My Rich Friend

My rich friend thought otherwise. Life is just a bunch of "plans". Do it right with appropriate actions, and favourable results can be had. They take full accountability for the way they act.

Conclusion:

When you keep on believing that life only happens to you, you eventually lose the power to change the things that control your life. My rich friend takes responsibility for whatever life brings because he knows it stems from his actions. My poor friend feels like the world is ONE MEAN BASTARD! If you want to gain financial success, think like my rich friend think like the best! Believe that your future is created by YOU and not by other people or events.

> **Rich People Focus on Opportunities; Poor People Focus on Problems**
>
> ▸ **Opportunities vs Obstacles**
> Rich people: views as opportunity to grow
> Poor people: views as hindrance to laid-back life
>
> ▸ **Action vs Complain**
> Rich people: spend little time complaining
> Poor people: squander time and energy
>
> ▸ **CONCLUSION: problems are 'molding process'. You either survive and thrive, or die and wither away.**
>
> ▸

2. My Rich Friend focuses on opportunities while My Poor Friend focuses on problems

There are so many opportunities in this world. Some opportunities smack us dead in the face, while others are not as straight forward. In order to see them all, understand that problems are opportunities that just need to be solved. When you see life through superficial lenses, you only see the façade and fail to appreciate the blessings that are really involved.

- ✓ **Opportunities versus Obstacles**

    My Poor Friend

    The difference between My Rich Friend and My Poor Friend is their attitudes toward a problem. When faced with a dilemma, My Poor Friend sees it as the end to his easy life. He loathes difficult situations and never really faces them. The more problems he faces, the more he views his life as complicated.

    My Rich Friend

    Rich people see problem as a door for new opportunities. They focus on solution rather than dawdle in despair. With every obstacle, they treat things positively and look beyond what is obvious. Rich people concentrate in finding solutions to their crisis. They elucidate things to see things at a better perspective.

- ✓ **Action versus Complain**

    My Poor Friend

    Poor people keep on complaining

about the obstacles. They squander time whining about the circumstances in their life. At the end of the day, their grumble intensifies since they have not done anything to solve the issue.

My Rich Friend

Rich people act on their problems. They may moan a little, but they work to unravel the misery. The more problems they solve, the better their feeling.

Conclusion

Problems and failures are part of your molding process to become tough and be a better person. With problems, you learn from your mistakes and do better when the next one comes. When you face an opportunity, you come up with creative solutions. Avoid the poor man's action of sitting down and staying cranky about it.

> **Rich People Have Big Dreams, Poor People Have Small Dreams**
>
> ▸ **Big vs Small**
> Rich people: sets intimidating goals
> Poor people: small dreams are easier to achieve and costs little
>
> ▸ **Aspirant vs Contentment**
> Rich people: aspires more
> Poor people: easily contented, conditioned to think that 'more is greedy'
>
> ▸

3. My Rich Friend dreams BIG while My Poor Friend dreams small.

Dreams are the picture to success. When a person dreams, he exerts effort to paint that picture on a canvass. Both My Rich Friend and My Poor Friend dream. The difference is the size of their dream. When you have small dreams, you work less whereas big dreamers work extra hard to achieve.

✓ **Big versus Small**

My Poor Friend

My Poor Friend has small dreams. That's like cutting your headlights on in pitch black darkness, but not your high beams. Seems like they are comfortable with a 9 to 5 and then retire. This is something that so many can achieve, My Poor Friend knows a lot of effort they do not need. Anyway, why work hard? They have achieved their dream after all.

My Rich Friend

My Rich Friend knows that to achieve Big things you must first dream big things! Wealthy people stick to that notion. They do not dream of being a 9 to 5'er just surviving. They dream of being a Chief Executive Officer striving and THRIVING. They do not look for jobs, they create jobs.

✓ **Aspirant versus Contentment**

My Poor Friend

Poor people get comfortable with what they have. They do not aspire for more they don't "go get the bag".

They believe that to desire more leads to complication. They are ok with whatever is going on, no matter the situation.

My Rich Friend

Rich people just aspire for higher heights. They know that their abilities can take them to bigger places in life. Because they have big dreams, they work hard to achieve and turn aspirations to reality.

Conclusion

How can you achieve BIG things if you do not first dream BIG things? Aspirations is turning dreams into a vision and it cost absolutely NOTHING to dream. So, you have nothing to lose.

> **Rich People Commit To Their Dreams; Poor People Dream Their Dreams**
>
> ▸ **The poor mind is conditioned** to just dream about dreams because they cost nothing, but the price is hard work if they want it to materialize.
>
> ▸ **The rich mind is committed** to not only dream big, but also take BIG action steps to get closer to the dream!
>
> ▸

4. My Rich Friend is committed to their dreams while My Poor friend sleep dreams their dreams

It is a proven fact, that dreams are the initial step, to achieving success. But that's not it, there is more needed to achieve it. In order to obtain your dream, you have to work hard to receive it

✓ **Commitment versus Dreaming**

My Poor Friend

Poor people love to dream even

when it is time to work. They dream of being a Boss, and all its wonderful perks. They keep on thinking how good it is to live in opulence, but they never do anything to try and experience it.

My Rich Friend

Rich people know that nothing happens if you do nothing. They know that nothing is going to happen overnight, but many nights compiled. They turn their dream into a vision, vision into a mission, and work hard by being consistent, dedicated and committed.

Conclusion

Dreaming big does not make you rich. You need to work hard when you set your goals. Small steps every day are better than just waiting for time to pass without action. At the end of the day, the small deeds can accumulate and lead you to the stairs of success.

> **Rich People Play to Win, Poor People Play NOT to Lose**
>
> ▸ **Poor people** play the game of life only just to prevent losing, thus 'play safe'
>
> ▸ **Rich People** are not or less afraid of losing, and understand that failing is part and parcel of success.
>
> ▸

5. My Rich Friend plays to win while My Poor Friend plays only not to lose money

Life is a gamble, ask yourself, "What's your purpose for playing?". Every decision is a risk, mindset is the biggest difference.

✓ **Risk-taker versus Playing Safe**

My Poor Friend

In the game of life, poor people play,

not to lose. They are too careful to invest and make sure that things turn out the way they want them to. When uncertainty arrives, they don't even decide. They always play it safe, attached to the stigma of failure and too afraid to make mistakes.

My Rich Friend

For rich people, life is about risk, but calculated. The risk that they take are never unsubstantiated. For them losing is not even an option, they study and analyze how things work and invest once the time is proper.

Conclusion

Only those who are willing to take risk achieve financial stability and abundance. The bigger the risk that you take, the bigger is your reward. However, even rich people do not jump to risks without preparation. When you are ready to take a risk, be sure that your preparation is enough to ensure winning. Be armed when you gamble with life.

> **Rich People Network with the Rich; The Poor with the Poor**
>
> ▸ **Receptivity vs hostility**
>
> ▸ **Poor people** think lowly of the rich, and believe that anything associated with 'rich' is filth, dirty, ill-gotten.
>
> ▸ **Rich People** understand that to attract wealth, who he spends most of his time with is the bottom-line.
>
> ▸ "What you focus on expands"!

6. My Rich Friend networks with other rich and successful people while My Poor Friend networks with other poor people.

Birds of a feather, flock together is not just some cliché terminology. This is very true and energy is transferable.

✓ **Receptivity versus hostility**

My Poor Friend

Poor people are hostile to rich people. They think that their lifestyle is not tolerable. Instead, they associate with people with the same income as theirs. They spend time wondering how rich people become richer and envy the luck they have.

My Rich Friend

Rich people are receptive to new ideas and new people. They spend time with people who can help them achieve their dreams. They join people earning six digits or more. They analyze how these wealthy people become richer and absorb their ways and thinking.

Conclusion

Poor people think that your wealth depends on your family origin. You are rich if only you belong to a family of rich. Rich people think otherwise. They go with people who can help them. They talk to financially successful people taking notes of their secrets to prosperity. With the right associations, you can become rich even when you come from poor family.

Rich People Are Good Learners; A Poor Person Says "I Know Everything"

▸ **The 3 most dangerous words: "I KNOW THAT".**

▸

7. My Rich Friend is a good learner while My Poor Friend thinks they know everything.

Life is all about learning. When you assert that, you know everything, learning stops. However, when you acknowledge that you still need more knowledge, you will yearn to learn even more.

- ✓ **Open-mindedness versus Close-mindedness**

   My Poor Friend

   Poor people believe that they know everything. They know how life works and how to live well. Their beliefs make them close their minds to new ideas. If you are not willing to learn, you will never know why rich people become richer and why remain poor despite all your efforts.

   My Rich Friend

   Rich people admit that they still need to learn. When you give a room for improvement and new ideas, you open your mind to possibilities. One of the easiest ways to financial abundance is to learn from people who achieved the status.

Conclusion:

The key to financial success is to accept your shortcomings and learn from people. To be the best, you need to learn from the best and learn to be the best. Only when you open up for learning can you live a life of abundance.

Rich People are Leaders while Poor People are Followers

▸ **REMEMBER:** even a dead fish can flow with the river flow!

▸ **You don't have to lead an army of employees; the first and most important to start leading is yourself.**

8. My Rich Friend is a Leader while My Poor Friend is a Follower

Most financially successful people lead the way. Being a leader, you are in front of the actions. Because of the courage needed to be a leader, only those with strong personality become the manager.

✓ **Leaders versus Followers**

My Poor Friend

Poor people have herd mentality. They like to follow where the water flows. Instead of taking the lead, they are happy to let others do the thinking. They do not want to take responsibility over their decisions. When somebody asks for their opinion, they pass it to others so as not to take the blame for failures later on.

My Rich Friend

Rich people take the initiative. They decide for themselves and take full responsibility for their decisions. They can work independently.

Conclusion

Rich people are leaders and leaders are rich people. This idea comes because of the independent attitude of leaders and rich people. Even if an ordinary office setting, the leaders are often responsible for the whole group. They may have bigger responsibilities, but they get higher pays too.

Rich People Focus on Saving while Poor People Concentrate on Spending

- Saving versus Spending

- Debit Card versus Credit Card

- Cautious versus Impulsive

9. My Rich Friend focuses on saving while My Poor Friend concentrates on spending

No matter how small or big your earning is, saving is a crucial part of becoming rich. If you try to save even ten dollars a day, that means 3,650 dollars a year and 36, 500 in ten years. Well that is even less the interest you get from the bank. Even if you earn 100,000 dollars a month but you also spend the whole amount, you will never get rich until your death.

- ✓ **Saving versus Spending**

    My Poor Friend

    Poor people usually spend more than what they earn. They do not believe in the value of savings. They earn 100 dollars and spend 110 dollars. In time, the excess expenditure piles up and before they know it, they are drowning in debt.

    My Rich Friend

    Rich people stays on a monthly and even daily budget. They spend only within their declared budget. They save a portion of their earning in the bank to earn further interest.

- ✓ **Debit Card versus Credit Card**

    My Poor Friend

    Poor people rely on credit cards. They cannot live without them. They dine out, shop and indulge to vacations using their plastic cards. Because they do not see the expenses and their cash remains intact, they feel that they are in complete control of their finances. Only to find out later on that everything is getting out of control.

My Rich Friend

Rich people do not purchase with credit cards. If they do not have cash, they use debit cards. They believe in the saying, "if you cannot afford it cash, you really cannot afford it".

✓ **Cautious versus Impulsive**

My Poor Friend

Poor people are impulsive buyers. They buy anything on sale, and anything discounted. Even if they do not need the items, they keep on buying thinking that they can save from the discounts.

My Rich Friend

Rich people think about the product many times before purchasing. They consider the affordability, quality and the usefulness of the item. When the item fails one of the criteria, they think about it repeatedly before finally deciding.

Conclusion

Earning money is hard. Because of the difficulty earning it, think twice or even thrice before you let go of your hard-earned income. No one knows the future, it is therefore important to save to ensure that you have something in case of drought.

> **Working for Money? Or Money Working For You?**
>
> ▸ **Poor people work for money** – trade in personal time, effort and get paid only when they work
>
> ▸ **Rich people work hard temporarily** – but invests their money in assets that in turn work hard to make money for them!
>
> ▸

10. My Rich Friend has their money work hard for them while My Poor Friend works hard for their money.

Everybody works hard. The way to let your money work for you is to know where to invest it. If you know where to put your investments, then you will make your money work hard for you.

✓ **Successful Investment versus Futile Investment**

My Poor Friend

Poor people keep on looking for money to come along. They keep on working and working to earn. They spend beyond their means and resort to loans that accumulate interest.

My Rich Friend

Rich people know where to invest their money. Instead of the banks charging them for credit card interest, they collect the interest of their savings. They experience a restful life while their money is working for them.

Conclusion

In order to stop working hard for your money as poor people do, live within your

means and save up. Let your money do the work and enjoy life.

> **SUMMARY**
>
> ▸ **You cannot change where and which family you are born in, or the circumstances you started out in**
>
> ▸ **But you are in control to alter your financial future!**
>
> ▸ **To think like a rich person is a trainable skill, just like anything else that requires learning!**

Summary

You cannot blame anyone born in a poor family. Maybe you can call that destiny. But to die still as poor as the rats, you blame only yourself. At an average, a man lives for 70 years. The approximately 25,550 days of your life is enough to make you rich. If you waste your days, destiny should not be the reason why you remained poor for the rest of your life.

The secret of millionaires is easy. They take each

day as a new beginning to face the challenges that will help them achieve their big dreams. Complaining is a total waste of time. Instead of comparing yourself with others, they work on their own lives. They take initiative rather than mere following. They are confident of their knowledge and skills and do not fear to take the risk.

Despite the destitute situation around us, money is in abundance. You can see money everywhere. It is just at the wrong place at the wrong time. To take advantage of the prosperity, be at the right place at the right time. Act. Find the opportunities to become rich.

Where can you classify yourself? Do you possess the mentality to become rich or negativities dominate your mind? Getting rich is very simple. All you need is the right attitude, mentality and action. With these characteristics, embarking the long and winding road to wealth is only a step away. Adapt the mentality of the rich and be rich; and otherwise, stay poor with the habits and mindset of the poor.

The 4 Essential Wealth Skills

It is probably silly to ask people who wants to be a millionaire. Without the need for further studies and research, the answer will be a resounding yes. Earning beyond what you need and spending on the things that you do not only need but also the things that you want are luxurious dreams of many. It is everyone's dream to trot around the world, send the children in esteemed universities, indulge in lavish pampering and donate to charities to help the poor. To take pleasure in all of these seems to be a distant ambition.

Everyone wants to be a millionaire. But the key to being one of the richest men in the world is to know the essentials to bring all the luck you need. Although there is no exact formula for richness, there are keys that will help you unlock the doors to success. It boils down to an effective system that rich and wealthy people apply. This should probably be very effective for them to live in luxury and their children's grandchildren. To employ the same skills will lose you nothing. Anyway, yes, you eat three times a day, but you barely fit in the trivial income your family has.

Before introducing the essential wealth skills, it is only proper to prepare you to your journey to prosperity. Like in any endeavor, you need to prepare and arm yourself with the anticipated needs. In trotting through the road of financial abundance, you must organize yourself. Here are the important things that you must bring with you as you move through the road to success.

V-P-U-C Cornerstones for Wealth Skill Building

- **Vision**

- **Plan**

- **Understanding**

- **Commitment**

Vision

The start of financial abundance is the vision you must set. As your vision gets bigger, your chance of becoming a millionaire is also bigger. Anyway, what is there that you must lose? To count the countless millions in your hands, you need to visualize yourself with hands on your fortune. Do you want a car, two cars or three? Do you want to have one successful business or an international business with branches all over the world? Think and imagine what your power can accommodate. Focus on the positive outcome of things and envision a comfortable and financially abundant life for you and your family. If you believe this will happen, it will. Otherwise, your doubts will keep you stationary.

Plan

Wealthy people do not just dream. They plan things and they do it specifically. They have a plan every day and they stick to it. They consider each day as a day to contribute to their future success. You just cannot leave your life to luck or as poor people see it, to destiny. Millionaires do not believe in predetermined fate. Instead, they hold responsible for their lives. They are in perfect control of their destiny. Instead of sitting down, they write all their goals and make a systematic wealth plan that they religiously follow.

Understanding

For you to reach your goal and set plans, you need to understand your whole situation. Look at your status at a wider perspective. Millionaires understand the flow of many in their hands. They know how much comes in and how much should they let go. Poor people only try to balance this flow. Sometimes they output is even higher than input. But for millionaires, their cash output is lower than their cash input. Therefore, they can save from their earnings.

Commitment

To become a millionaire, you must be committed to your dreams. Earning millions need a lot of effort and commitment. Remember, the road to financial abundance is not very easy.

There will be myriad of obstacles. If you have little commitment to your dream, you can quickly give up when you stumble.

Here are the essential things that you must bring with you along the road to millions. If you are ready to take a major turn in your life, read on below to know the secrets of those sleeping in luxury. Be ready to assess your own life and take action to make a change. As you read the article, you will be surprised to know that all you need to have are four wealth skills and you are ready to commence the journey to prosperity. Now, let us see if you can reach the end of the road.

WEALTH SKILL #1: Making Money from Scratch

- **Selling (commodities and products)**
  Garage
  Real Estate
  Commissioning

- **Offer Your Service**

- **NEW: Go Online! (start an Internet-based Business)**

WEALTH SKILL #1: Making Money from Scratch

It may be quite skeptical to become a millionaire from scratch. But it is true. Many rich men started from nothing.

Unlike other people who have a thick check book, plentiful savings and many properties to liquidate to start up a business, you are probably thinking that you can never be a candidate to become a millionaire. However, you do not need all these. All you need is yourself. You are the biggest and most indispensable asset of your future business. There are many known ways to make money from scratch. If you think this is impossible, then look around. Most successful people started out of scratch. All you need to do is to let your imagination work, be creative and confident.

1. Selling

Garage Sale

Selling is the traditional way of making money from scratch. You can sell your stuffs especially your second-hand things, junks or other odds. Instead of keeping the items in your storeroom, you can turn these into cash.

When you do this, you will be one of those who will say, "There is money in trash."

Real Estate

If you have a good communication skill, then, you have the power to convince people with your words and your words can be your best asset. Many successful real estate entrepreneurs started from scratch. With only their voice and words as starting capital, they were able to create millions.

Commissioning

Aside from real estate, you can also sell of other people's products. You can offer selling their stuffs along with your own. In return, you can get commission for every item sold.

Selling gives you unlimited source of funds. If you are industrious in dealing with different people, it is a sure hit. However, since you work in a customer related environment, be sure to have a lot of patience. You will meet people with varied personalities that will test your character. But do not get into them. Keep in mind that they can be your potential key to success.

If you are into selling, you must be always on the go. If your business calls for it, you need to be where the action is. Time flexibility is very crucial since many clients do not want to wait and there are many competitors out there yearning to earn as much as you do. Although it may seem to be a tough start up, you will gain the fruit of your efforts as you create a name for yourself. When that happens, you can be the boss of your own company.

2. Offer your Service

Each person has a unique skill to offer. The secret to making money from scratch is by taking advantage of your uniqueness. You can stand out from the crowd when you show your exceptional ability, talent or skill. To turn your skill into cash, offer your service to others. Advertise yourself and keep your customers satisfied to ensure a repeat customer or referral from others. Aside from the usual forms of advertisements, do not forget to charm people. Millionaires have a certain charm that draws people to them. As you bring more people closer to your services, your very own company will be a multi-million worth in no time.

Offering services is not only easy money. It also serves as an outlet for your talents, skills and abilities. Remember, you were not here to keep your uniqueness within. You must share it to the world and make it known. It does not only improve you, it also benefits other people.

The whole idea is to look for problems of clients and find solution to those problems. If people worry about broken things, fix them. As long as you find a solution for their most common problems and needs, then you will never lose your business market.

3. Go Online!

With the advent of online businesses, you do not need to go out of your own comforts just to get a six-figure income. You can earn money right form your home as long as you have internet access. When you are online, the possibilities of making money from scratch are endless. Money is just under your nose and only one click away. The good thing with online job is you get to stay at home, with no bosses and still you earn better than those working within the bounds of their office. Here are the common online money-making jobs.

Online Blogging

Online blogging started out as a hobby of people. It was their outlet on their emotions and everyday sentiments. However, as people relate to your own stories, you acquire followers that contribute to your blogs. As your blogs increase in number, visitors come and interact with you. When online advertisers see the increase in traffic in your site, they begin to ask for an ad space, and this can be your chance to earn income from something that started out as a hobby.

Article Writing

People use the internet as their primary source of information. This is the reason why online marketers require huge amount of information to satisfy the majority of online searchers. However, not all people have the time and talent to write and this is where you can come in. You can write for somebody and get payment for it.

Making money from scratch is tough. Your capital is only yourself. However, do not worry; you have the best starting capital that even big companies do not have. In investing huge amount of money, you also risk a lot. However, when you start from scratch, you have nothing to lose and everything to gain. It may be quite challenging, but the rewards are gratifying. If you want your first million now, you can have it right away. It is your own pace and no one will dictate how much or how little you can earn.

WEALTH SKILL #2: Budgeting Your Money

▸ **Provides Insights**

▸ **Teaches Self-Control**

▸ **Organizes your Finance**

▸ **Offer New Opportunities**

▸ **Provide More Cash Flow Money**

WEALTH SKILL #2: Budgeting Your Money

In the first part of the article, it mentioned about understanding your money. If you want to be a millionaire, you need to learn the wealth skill number two, budgeting your money. Rich people do not spend more than what they earn. Instead, they religiously keep a portion of it and let it earn interest. To follow their footsteps, you learn to manage your finances. Unless you learn this important skill, you will never reach the road to financial abundance.

Importance of Budgeting your Money

Provides Insights

Budgeting your money gives you knowledge of your earnings and spending. When you a basic knowledge of the whereabouts of your money, you create financial stability which is the crucial step to abundance.

Teaches Self-Control

When you know how to budget your

money, you develop self-discipline. You are able to control your finances and avoid unnecessary expenses. Learning to budget makes you the boss of your money instead of being a slave to your finances.

Organizes your Finance

Organizing your finances warns you for any potential financial problem. Your budget can serve as a record of all your financial transactions, guide for paying utility bills and immediately warns you when you overspend.

Offer New Opportunities

When you know how to budget your money, you can grab opportunities that you may otherwise miss. Because you know the flow of money, you can exactly determine if you have excess funds to invest to other moneymaking opportunities.

Provide More Cash Flow Money

The greatest benefit of budgeting your money is having extra money. When you cut unnecessary payments like penalties and late interests, you can save up for your future needs. When you pay your bills on time, you not only avoid late charges but also create a good name for yourself and your company.

Earning your first million is challenging and budgeting it according to your needs is more challenging. The key to being rich is to be in control of your finances.

>   **Tips to Budget your Money**
>   - **Make a List**
>
>   - **Separate your Money**
>   Working Budget
>   Savings
>   Spending Money

Knowing the benefits of budgeting is futile if you do not practice it. To arm you with the competence needed in Wealth skill number 2, here are the tips to help you stay within the budget.

Tips to Budget your Money

Make a List

When you receive your first million, keep it a habit to make a list of the things that you need to pay. Determine your future expenses and set aside funds for your needs. If you run a business, make sure you separate the working budget of your company. These include money for purchasing, maintenance and salary of your employees. If you do not have a company and only works for yourself or for others, know your expenditures until the next payday comes. Write specifically each item and opposite each, its corresponding amount. This way, you will know whether you are still within your budget or you are exceeding from your earnings.

Separate your Money

For people who are very impulsive when it comes to spending, separating the budget into parts is ideal. You can allocate your funds based on the following:

✓ **Working Budget**

Your working budget includes your daily or monthly expenses. Usually, this comprises the biggest share in the budget. This is where you will get the payment for your monthly bills, food, allowance and transportation.

✓ **Savings**

No matter how small your income, savings should be a part of your budget. To be wealthy means to save more than what you spend. Even a meager earner can become rich as long as you save enough for your future. The savings must comprise at least 20% to 30% of your monthly budget.

✓ **Spending Money**

Of course, life will be boring if you only work to live and save. Your monthly leisure activities must be a part of your budget. As the cliché goes, "All work with no play, makes a boy a dull one." Working is more rewarding and fun if you get to treat yourself occasionally. You can get the money for your new clothes, vacation or pampering yourself from the spending money. To avoid overspending, make sure to leave your debit and credit cards at home and stay strictly within your spending money.

> **WEALTH SKILL #3: Making More Money with Money**
> - Invest
> - Save in Banks
> - Offer Loans

WEALTH SKILL #3: Making More Money with Money

Once you have your millions, you can become richer by comfortably sitting at home and letting your money do the work. Millionaires are richer not because they work hard to earn their millions but because they let their money work hard for them. If you are on the way to financial abundance, here are the proven ways to let your money do the work for you.

Invest

Investing is the wisest way to make your money work. However, wise investment is important for you to keep your money working. Before you invest, make sure you have the knowledge of the field where you want to invest. Invest in properties that appreciate in time like real estate properties and stocks. Do not invest in appliances, electronics or even automobiles. These things depreciate through time. This means instead of making more money out of your money, you end up with less.

Save in Banks

If you have extra amount of money, you can deposit it in banks. You can keep it safely and earn interest at the same time. Although the interest is not much, at least it earns compared when you keep it in your home. Other banks can give as high as 3% interest per annum. Time deposits earn more compared to ordinary savings account. The disadvantage of time deposit is you have to allow your investment to mature before you can withdraw your money.

Offer Loans

Many people and small companies need money to start their own business or meet the ends of their financial status. When you help these people with their financial needs, you can charge them with interest. Just be careful when you give loans to people. Make sure they have the paying capacity to ensure your money's return or better yet ask for collaterals.

WEALTH SKILL #4: Protecting Your Money

- Insurance

- Be a Wise Investor

WEALTH SKILL #4: Protecting Your Money

Once you have the millions, you know how to budget and you keep the money working for you, the next thing that you should do is to protect your money. Protecting your money is important for you and your grandchildren to enjoy the luxurious life. Without appropriate guarding, you can be a one-day millionaire and live in poverty the next day.

Insurance

Insurance guards your investments and money. Like when you insure your house and other assets, you safeguard your properties from misfortunes. When you invest your money, keep them in banks with good insurance policies. Most banks guarantee deposits up to $100,000 per person. In that amount, it is wise to spread your money across many banks to get the best from insurance. The insurance does not only hold true to your money in banks but also to your other assets.

Be a Wise Investor

Your millions are your hard earnings. It is the fruit of your precious time and effort. Therefore, before you invest your money, understand the market where you will put it. A wise investor makes a research of the in and out of the business. You can do direct observation or work with a person known to be expert in the field.

CONCLUSION

The road to wealth is challenging. Nevertheless, if you have the four essential wealth skills, everything will be easy. Remember, you can make money from scratch but once you have it, learn to budget your money, make it work for you and protect it. Although wealth does not come overnight, you can start adapting and mastering the skills now. The earlier you start with the skill, the earlier you become rich.

7 Key Ways to Change Tomorrow, Today

The future is a manifestation of the present deeds. You can know your future by your present actions. You can transform your future by changing your present life. However, change is one of the most difficult things to experience. Many people cannot tolerate drastic changes in their lives. Because of the uncertainties that come with change, people are reluctant with it. If you want to change your tomorrow, you need to commence the changes today. Here are the 7 vital steps to help you bring a more fruitful tomorrow.

#1: You Are the Sum of the 5 People You Spend Most Of Your Time With

- The people around you have direct influence on your life

- The person you are with can elevate you as much as they can pull you down

- Identify the 5 people you spend most of your time with and their qualities

- **What attitudes do you share with these 5 people in your life?**

#1: You Are the Sum of the 5 People You Spend Most Of Your Time With

If you want to know your future, look at the lives of the people you are presently with. The people around you have direct influence on your life. You acquire some of their attitudes, principles and practices. You are like a small child that imbibes the practices of the adults around. When you go with dishonest people, eventually you alter your own values and acquire their dishonesty. However, if you go for honest people, their honesty reinforces your own personal values. The kinds of people you share your life with are very powerful personalities that affect your present actions and later own your future life. Because of their great impact in your life, it is very crucial that you know them very well. Once you know their influence on you, you will know how to take it to your own advantage.

The idea of being the sum of the people around you is often one of the most neglected parts of human psychology. Although this is not a novel thinking, people keep on ignoring the bearing of others in their lives. As a result, they just end up being like their detested character. This is all because they spent too much time with the person. The person you are with can elevate you as much as they can pull you down. The first step to change your future today is by knowing the five people from your core circle. For you to see their impact in your life, here are the steps that you can do.

Identify the Five people you spend most of your time with

Because you are the sum of the people around you, you need to be careful with the people you spend most of your time with. Although some of them are indispensable in your life, like your parents or siblings, try to spend as little time as possible to inevitable people with negative impact for your future life. Other people that you may frequently spend your time with are your friends, office mates or schoolmates and your special someone. Each person may have a different answer to the five people they spend most of their time with. But it will mostly revolve around these groups.

Identify the Qualities of these Five People

Once you have identified the five people in your life, try to assess each one's personality. Look at them at every aspect of their life. Look at their family relationship, their dedication to work or school, their attitude towards problems and their outlook in life. Getting to know these people will help you know yourself better.

Identify the attitudes you share with these five people in your life

After knowing your core circle and their special attributes, try to assess your own life. What positive and negative characteristics do you possess? To whom can you relate your characteristics? When you are able to identify the major influence in that character trait, then you can do something about it. If you want to enhance a positive attribute coming from one of your core groups, then try to get closer to the person. The more time you spend with him/her, the better you can imitate that attitude. However, if you see mostly negative attributes to your core group, better reconsider your relationship with the person.

Everyone needs a tribe. However, your tribe must exert a good influence in your life to benefit from it. If you are in the bad company, your future is at risk. Your choices today including your choice of company have a direct effect on your life. If you want to know your future, look at the lives of the people you spend most of your life with.

#2: Find a Mentor
- Acts as a Role Model
- Willingness to Share
- Motivates Others

#2: Find a Mentor

Everyone look up to someone, it may be an old teacher, your parent or elder sister or brother or your very own best friend. The person you admire may serve as your mentor. Because you adore him/her, most likely you listen to his/her suggestions and teachings. A good mentor provides new knowledge and directs you to the right path. If you wish to change your life tomorrow, look for a good mentor who will bring you to the kind of life you wish to have. To whether your mentor is good for keeping, here are the ideal characteristics of a mentor.

Acts as a Role Model

You have to practice what you teach. To be an effective mentor, you need to do what you say. The best way to direct a person in the right path is by modelling a good example. As the cliché goes, actions speak louder than words. If your mentor is worthy of emulation, look at his/her life. Otherwise, you must find other mentors to relate your life with.

Willingness to Share

A good mentor is willing to share the secrets of good life. If your mentor is open to share his/her expertise and teaches you the skills to succeed in life, you can trust the person with your life.

Motivates Others

A good mentor can bring out the intrinsic motivation in a person. For your mentor to be a good leader, he/she must bring out the best in you. Some students or followers go back to their old ways when the mentor disappears. If you are one of these people, your mentor is not effective. An effective mentor naturally brings out the inner motivation in his followers. Even in his absence, the followers stay within his teachings without the need for constant supervision.

> **#3: Start or Join a Team of Like-Minded Individuals**
> - Provides a Sense of Security
> - Increased Learning
> - Compensate to an individual's weakness
> - Develop a Personal Relationship
> - Increased Understanding of other people's perspective

#3: Start or Join a Team of Like-Minded Individuals

A group's effort is stronger than an individual's effort. When you want to transform your life today, join groups or teams with the same interest as yours. Unlike when you are working alone to change some aspects of your life, a group effort is stronger and harder to disrupt. When you belong to a team, your conviction to better life is tougher and thus harder to break. When you reach a saturation point, your team can assist and support you along the journey. Contrary to working alone, the team with like-minded individuals can back you up when you lose your perseverance. Below are the advantages of working as a team.

Provides a Sense of Security

Working as a team gives you a feeling of security. When you have a group, who shares the same interest as yours, you are sure of their support with any problem that may come. You know that there are people who stay with you and will guide you as you go along.

Increased Learning

As you work with people, you increase your knowledge with their experiences. Because you share common interest, you can draw wisdom from them. You do not have to experience things personally just to learn. By listening to their sentiments, you can learn a lot from the events in their lives.

Compensate to an individual's weakness

Each person has his own weakness. When you work alone to change your future, even the small weakness can be deleterious to your goal. However, if you have a team, other members can compensate for your own weakness. They can assist you to deal with a weakness and teach you how to overcome it. You can draw strength from the team, especially in your lowest situation.

Develop a Personal Relationship

Joining a team also provides you with relationships that are more personal. As you spend more time with your team, you can find friendship with them and influence each other. Again, in this case, we go back to the five people you spend most of your time with. Make sure that the team you will join will have a positive impact in your future life.

Increased Understanding of other people's perspective

Because you are working with other people, you will have a better understanding on the way people think and act. You can use your learning to assess your own character and later improve yourself.

#4: Get Into Business
- **Be your Own Boss**
- **Flexible Time**
- **Generate Unlimited Income** (be paid based on what you are truly worth rather than what your boss thinks you are worth)

#4: Get Into Business

Most people who want to transform their lives start with a business. If you notice, the richest people are not employees, but they are entrepreneurs who took the risk to do things on their own. If you want to achieve a better financial status in the future, you can begin establishing your own business today. Here are the perceived benefits of having your own business.

Be your Own Boss

If you are an employee, you need to get along with your boss and your co-workers. There are too many people to work with. You need to adapt to their personality and whims. When you have your own business, you become your own boss. You do not have to adapt to anyone's caprice. All you need to do is work hard and work with your future clients.

Flexible Time

Working in an office means spending 8 hours in the area. You cannot leave the workplace since sanctions are ready for implementation. When you have your own business, you can own your time. You have the final say about your day off, working hours and your break time.

Generate Unlimited Income

Because you work on your own pace, you can generate more income as you wish. Unlike when you are an ordinary employee, you only receive your pay checks twice and at a predicted amount. In business, you can generate millions within days or years depending on your own capacity.

> #5: Start a Bank Account for Investing Purpose
>
> ▸ Starting a bank account helps you save your resources and invest for your purpose

#5: Start a Bank Account for Investing Purpose

Starting a bank account helps you save your resources and invest for your purpose. Instead of keeping your money in your hands, having a bank account gives you countless of benefits. Here are the few advantages of maintaining a bank account.

Safer

When you have your bank account, you do not personally keep your money. The bank holds responsibility to your money. Therefore, you safeguard it from thieves and possible disasters like natural and man-made calamities. Even during a bankruptcy, your money has insurance to keep the depositor's worry free.

Easier to Save

Banks help you save money. Most people who overspend keep more cash with them. When you keep your money in the banks, you avoid too much spending. You also avoid withdrawing large amount of money in banks because of their existing withdrawal limits.

You Earn Interest

With bank accounts, your money works for you. If you keep your money in your own safekeeping, the value is the same from day one up to the day you will need it. If you keep it in banks, it becomes your personal investment because you earn interest every month.

> #6: How To Get More Time In A Day To Build Your Financial Freedom
> - Prioritize things
> - Know your most productive hours
> - Start and finish your task
> - Analyze your situation
> - Create a goal
> - Delegate and outsource
> - Use your waiting time productively

#6: Time Management: How To Get More Time In A Day To Build Your Financial Freedom

Sometimes you can hear people say that 24 hours in a day is not enough to finish all their work and meet all the deadlines. If you are one of these people, you will hear answers like "if you cannot find time, make time." With the busy society that you are in, it feels that you need to compress everything in 24 hours. The secret to meeting your set goals is simply by ceasing to complain and sit down and start doing the work. Most people who keep on saying time is not enough are the people who love to complain. Instead of using the time working, they spend two or three hours complaining and discerning how to start the work. If others can compress all their obligations in the time given to them, why cannot you do it?

Time Management

The key to keeping up with your deadlines is through efficient time management. With the right allocation of your time and task, you can meet your target and still find time to relax. Although time management is a skill, you can learn it as you practice it. Here are some of the proven beneficial time management tips.

Prioritize things

You can start your day by listing the things you need to accomplish prioritizing those that are urgent. When you have a to-do-list, you can keep your mind focused on your list and prevent straying away from this. You can create the list by writing down those that need your immediate attention. Once you finish the most urgent one, you can start doing the next in line and so on. By prioritizing things, you prevent sacrificing a task over another.

Know your most productive hours

Different people have different levels of productivity during the day. Although most people are more productive in the morning, there are also people who find the restful afternoons to work at their best. If you are a morning person, try to delegate complicated task in the morning. When you know your most productive hours, you can allot this time to accomplish difficult work and set aside the easier ones during your idle moments.

Start and finish your task

The problem with people who complains of insufficient time is leaving a task unfinished and starting a new work. If you want to adapt a good time management skill, finish all tasks that you have started. Otherwise, your day will be over with several tasks open and hanging. In the end, you do not accomplish even a small work and you will totally screw up everything.

Examine your situation

If you feel running after the clock each day, it is time to sit down and analyze the whole situation. There might be problems on the way you handle your time. Find out activities where you spend too much of your time. Once you discover these, then you can be more watchful when doing them. If you waste three to five hours surfing social network sites, you can reduce this to one hour to make the remaining hours more productive.

Create a goal

A goal is your motivation to time management. When you set your goals, be realistic. Remember that you only have 24 hours in a day. Never set goals that are not feasible. Otherwise, you will end up frustrated every day.

Delegate and outsource

There is nothing wrong in volunteering your services to people. However, be realistic. You cannot be a hero every day. Learn to delegate other task to trusted people and let them take responsibility for it. Much as you would want to do everything, multi-tasking is often difficult. If you are not good at it, you will end up sacrificing some things over another.

Use your waiting time productively

Waiting is one of the most time-wasting activities. You wait for your turn in the cashier's line, wait for the food service and wait for a long line in the department stores. You can spend these hours of waiting productively. Instead of watching the next leaf to fall or the next person who will enter the door, you can bring a good book to read or check papers or bring any handy task with you. As you learn to do this, the number of tasks you finish during your waiting times can save you from many obligations.

Time management is learning to use your time wisely and to your own advantage. It is a skill that no one teaches you, but you need to learn to survive the challenges in life. For as long as you are keeping your things well organized, you are in control of your time and your life.

#7: Focus On One Project At A Time!

- Break things into bite sized chunks
- Remove possible distractions
- Keep your goals clear

#7: Focus On One Project At A Time!

Our brains are like computers. When you put several tasks all at the same time, the computer hangs and breaks down. Like computers, our brain can only fully accommodate one project at a time. Although some people believe in multi-tasking, the quality of product produced from multi-tasking is not as efficient as the project produced with full focus. This is because your brain can only focus on a single thought at a time. When you follow the concept of one project at a time, your output is superior and is more likely to be completed.

Staying focus on one project and closing your thoughts from other tasks is quite difficult. The presence of constant distractions in the environment and in your mind can easily divert your attention to other things. No matter how difficult the skill is, you need to master it to create changes in your life that will be beneficial for your future. To help you learn the skill, here are the tips that you must follow.

Break things into bite sized chunks

Do not overwhelm yourself with huge task. If you can break it into smaller tasks, much better. Split difficult task in several smaller and attainable projects. Instead of getting an overpowering project, try to divide it into divisions.

Remove possible distractions

You work best in a quiet environment; find a quiet room where you can focus on your project. Avoid distractions like noise, interruptions and other forms of disturbances.

Keep your goals clear

One of the best ways to stay focused in a project is by making your goals clear. When you have clear goals, all will direct all your effort to attain the goal you set. It is easier to keep you motivated when you have realistic and attainable goals.

Conclusion

The future is a manifestation of the present deeds. You can know your future by your present actions. You can transform your future by changing your present life. However, change is one of the most difficult things to experience. Many people cannot tolerate drastic changes in their lives. Because of the uncertainties that come with change, people are reluctant with it. If you want to change your tomorrow, you need to commence the changes today. Here are the 7 vital steps to help you bring a more fruitful tomorrow.

Making Money Online For Beginners

You know, it's funny. I took an entire year off from marketing online and yet I can still come back and easily make money, even in a crowed "niche" like Internet marketing.

Why?

Am I any smarter than you? I'd like to think so, but probably not. The only reason why I can take so much time off, miss so many "new" developments on how to market online and still easily jump right back into business just like I never left is simple.

I work from a different perspective than most people do. You should already have a clear sense of that from reading this book. Making money does not have to be complicated.

You just have to work from the right frame of mind.

Really all it takes is a little shift in the way you think, and you'll start to see opportunities where you never saw them before.

With this section of the book it is my intention to give you a new frame of mind to work from and hopefully it will give you a renewed sense of purpose because you'll know without a doubt that money is just a few hours worth of work/planning away.

Evergreen Marketing Secrets You Can Take To The Bank

Before I get into the heart of this section, I want to make sure you completely understand the direction I'm taking.

I have nothing against giving you specific techniques and strategies because they are important, but they are never more important than the thought process that went into creating them.

Evergreen marketing secrets refers to the fact that I'm giving you proven concepts (that never stop working) based on the nature of the people you sell to. People can change a lot of things about themselves, but their nature isn't usually one of them. People can go against their nature (for short periods of time) but rarely can they change it.

In the future you should make a conscious effort to try and understand why something is done instead of just copying what you see someone else successfully doing. There is always something more beneath the surface that you can study and learn from.

The concepts I'm going to reveal help you to tap into the minds of the people you want money from.

People will almost never give you their money for your reasons. What you have to do is show people that you want their money for the exact same reasons they want to give their money to somebody/anybody and believe it or not, that's a lot easier to do than it sounds.

Once you understand how to see what motivates another person, you can put yourself in position to show them how what you have to offer will help them do whatever it is they're trying to do. That's really the only way to get someone's attention.

Don't try to convince people they need what you're selling.

Show them how what you're selling will help them do something they're already trying to do. That makes your product a natural fit for what they care about.

People care about themselves first, what they're trying to do, anyone else who seems to care about them and anything that appears to be able to help them do more of what they already want to do.

What I just said will become much clearer as you read the rest of this section of the book. You will completely understand exactly what to say to people and how to structure your product offers in a way that's most attractive to the people you want money from.

The Basic Truth About Success

I'm about to address one of the biggest obstacles standing in the way of you making money right now.

Being successful at anything you choose to do requires hard work and consistency. I know that in the Internet marketing field, use of those words is a big no-no, but it's the undeniable truth.

Without an understanding that you may have to work for your success you might think there's some secret formula out there that's going to magically put money in your pockets simply because you know it.

Knowing this, I titled this section "Making Money Online for Newbies" because it implies that everything else you've been doing is hard and that I've found some simple "secret" you aren't aware of.

It was a very direct way to get your attention and I'm not the only marketer who understands that.

All you have to do is look at how many products you've bought with the expectation that if you bought it, you would be able to turn your business around with the "new secrets" you thought you were going to learn to see I'm telling the truth.

I know you've seen some people who have hit the net full speed with their first product and had all kinds of crazy success.

Many times it's a fluke and it's not something that person can ever reproduce because since their first product launch did so well, they get trapped into thinking that what they did was easy, forgetting all they time and effort they put into everything that got them there.

It's easy to get trapped into thinking that success is easy if you just have the right "knowledge" on your side. That's the big myth pushed on you by slick marketers who only want to sell you stuff.

But the truth of the matter is success doesn't always come easy even if you know the best "secrets" out there.

Anytime I need money, there are always a few basic concepts I can rely on that will always produce profits in a short amount of time without me having to spend any money on advertising.

The only reason I know about these concepts is because I read pretty much everything I could get my hands on until one day things just started to make sense, but it wasn't easy to get to this point.

When I started out I had no real money, no business or online marketing background, no support from my family or friends, no computer knowledge

That's not the easiest way to start but I didn't care. I wanted to be my own boss and be in control of my own life as much as possible.

Periodt.

Now, making money online isn't a dream for me anymore simply because I refused to let anything stand in the way of what I wanted. It did take me a few solid years to start making money however.

The most important thing I've learned about what it takes to be successful is that you can't give up. Ever. Success has a way of waiting until 99.9% of the people who were looking for it give up in frustration before it decides to show up at your feet.

It's A Test Designed To See Who's Worthy

"Perseverance is the blossomed fruit from the roots of consistency which lies in the garden of success."

If you want to have a better business, or you want to make more money, or you want better things for yourself and for your family, "What Are You Doing About It?"

Sitting back and wishing is easy.

Criticizing other people for having the kind of success you want for yourself is dangerous and so easy to do it's scary.

Sitting back and complaining that no one is around to help you is even easier. It's always easy to give yourself an excuse for not doing what you know needs to be done.

Doing everything you can to make your dreams a reality and humbling yourself to ask for help when it's needed are where most people fall flat. Everything you need to get your business to where you want it to be can be found if you're willing to look hard enough.

When I couldn't get support and understanding from my family (instead of getting discouraged and giving up) I turned to marketers who understood this "crazy need" I have to work for myself and were willing to help.

When I didn't have a clue how to write HTML I took every tutorial that popped up in the search engines.

When I didn't even have $10 to spare for advertising I learned (out of necessity) how to get thousands of targeted visitors a month to my sites for free.

You have obstacles in your way, which may seem insurmountable at times, but they aren't.

You may have family or "friends" who give you a hard time because they don't understand why you would want to put yourself through all frustration of trying to be your own boss. But in the end, most of them admire you for trying to do something they're afraid to do which is to potentially risk your financial security in the pursuit of it.

The Myth Of Effortless Success

How many moneymaking, supposedly life-altering packages have you bought in the last few months or years?

Do you now have the success you bought those packages to achieve?

Maybe you do or maybe you don't.

I'll let you in on a little secret. Almost anyone can make money using any of the moneymaking packages you'll find on the net.

People do it every single day.

The reason is because they understand that nothing magical will happen just because they bought the latest and greatest do all/be all, either get it or your life will be ruined product of the century.

These people understand that consistent effort is what will set them apart from the thousands who get nothing from the very same products they use to make more in a month than most people make in a year. You would be surprised to know the kind of money some people are making with simple products that others say are worthless.

It's your mentality that counts. How you think about the world around you determines your reality in it. Not everyone walking around on this planet operates from the same reality you do.

People with failing businesses "know" it's hard to get to the top and people at the top "know" it's easy for anyone to get to the top if they're willing to work hard on the right things to get there.

Many of the obstacles holding you back were placed there by you and what you believe to be true. A lot of times, you may be the one who is creating the very "rut" you complain about being in.

Now right about now you're probably saying, "Where does he get off telling me I'm standing in my own way of success" but really I'm saying a lot more than that.

It's not really your fault because you're probably blind to the truth. Working hard is only part of the equation.

You can try twisting a screw into a board with your fingers as hard as you can all day long, but I think you'd probably be better of using a screwdriver. In other words, working hard in the wrong way won't get anything done even though there's the appearance of action.

Time To Take Off The Tunnel Vision Glasses

We Internet marketers tend to get tunnel vision and only see other Internet marketers when we want to learn what to do.

The problem is that the Internet marketer(s) you choose to learn from likely learned from other Internet marketers who (you guessed it) learned from other Internet marketers.

Dan Kennedy calls this marketing incest and it could be the biggest reason why your success has been put on hold.

What I mean by marketing incest here is doing what every other marketer is doing instead of thinking for yourself.

Is There Anything You Can Do About it?

Of course. There's always something you can do about everything in any situation. May not always be your first choice but you can always do something.

One thing I do is spend time looking for products I'm interested in (anything not related to Internet marketing) just to see how other businesses in markets not related to mine try and sell me their goods. That's how I came up with one of my main concepts.

Think about this.

Let's say you have a tractor, and you use it to work your farm, which is what produces the income you live off of.

When your tractor wears out a part (and it will) seeing as how it is the vehicle you consistently use to put food on the table, wouldn't you go out and look for a store that sells the part(s) you need?

Yeah, you would.

Ok, now when you walk into the store, do the salespeople need to sell you on the benefits of getting your tractor fixed?

No.

You already knew the benefits before you walked through the door. You already have money in your hands and are looking to give it to the first sales person who finds the part you need to help you get back to doing what you already want to do.

Make sense?..... If not, everything will get a lot clearer in a minute.

The Easy Way To Find Money

I'm not much of a fan of working hard. I'll do it, but only if I don't have a choice. That being said, I find myself working surprisingly hard trying to find the easiest ways to do things and that's the reason I put this section in the book.

To save you some of the time and effort I've put into working hard to be lazy and still make money online.

What I've found is that even though you may know at least as much as some of your biggest competitors about making money, the reason you may not bank the kind of sales figures they do has a lot to do with a massive amount of leverage.

Leverage is when you can put the efforts of 100's or even 1,000's of other people behind you so they can help push you forward to do things you couldn't do on your own.

Think about it.

When was the last time you got an email from a "guru" about his latest product and didn't get at least ten other messages from that "guru's" affiliates telling you about the exact same product?

Am I telling you to create your own product and start an affiliate program?

No.

That's too much work.

What I want you to understand is that many of your more successful competitors understand something that guides most of the actions they take in business.

What's that?

Why work hard by yourself when you can get other people to work hard for you as well?

How does that mindset apply to you?

Simple.

You should never do anything online that doesn't multiply your efforts on a project even after you stop putting any of your time and energy into it. Your time is limited to 24 hours in a day but 100's of people can put thousands of combined hours into promoting you.

The basic idea:

If someone is running full speed at you, is it easier to stand your ground and try to stop them when they run into you or get behind them and push them forward?

Since they're already moving forward, it only makes sense that you'd have an easier and less painful time pushing them in the direction they're already headed in.

Right?

I'll give you an example.

Let's say you start getting a lot of emails promoting one new product in particular and this product seems to have a lot of buzz (negative or positive it doesn't matter) and affiliates behind it.

Many of the people I speak to tell me they simply delete emails like that (because they see those emails as being annoying) and all I can do is smile to myself because I know what emails like that really are.

Easy money.

Remember what I said about how easy it is to help people move in the direction they're already headed in? Well, if people have their minds completely made up to promote a particular product then why not help them find more ways to do it?

You could for example create (or hire someone to create) a simple series of 5-7 articles promoting that product and then sell the reprint rights to your email series at $10-20 a pop.

Sell just 50 copies of your eCourse and you've made $500-$1,000 for something that should only take you a day or two in setup time.

You don't have to worry about researching a niche, creating a huge product, managing affiliates, setting up joint ventures or any of that. And, you can set it all up so that Paypal.com pays you immediately whenever you make a sale because instant cash is always great.

The best part is that you don't have to find out if there's a demand for your information because you can clearly see that there is just from the sheer number of places you see promoting the product you're going to create an email series to endorse.

All people really want is an easy way to do more of what they've already set their mind on doing.

Sign up for as many newsletters as you want and whenever you get a flood of emails promoting a particular product, instead of getting mad and rushing to the delete button, just smile and remember what I said. Help people go where they're already trying to go.

Pretty much anyone interested in promoting the product you're getting all the emails on will snatch up the reprint rights to your email series without a long sales letter or any heavy convincing.

They're already headed in a particular direction and will see your product offering as a "vehicle" to help them get there faster.

Two easy ways to get traffic to your offer...

☐ Send out an email to your list announcing that you have a new email series for sale promoting a new product they're probably already interested in.

☐ Contact publishers and offer them reprint rights to your email course for free. The reason this is a good idea is because you'll be building a list you can send out your next offer to so it's worth giving your email course away to people who can reach thousands of other people who will be interested in your future offers.

Just make sure your emails link back to your site through

your copyright notice at the bottom.

The beauty of this idea is that you can do it several times a month and every time you do, you build a list of people who will look forward to the next email series you create. You would be able to make money whenever you wanted with a few simple emails to your list.

If you're interested in putting a little more effort into this you could create a monthly membership site where you offer promotional tools for the latest products to hit the market.

It's up to you. You can put as little or as much effort into this strategy as you want and still make it work for you. Opportunities for profit are literally everywhere you look if you consistently keep an open mind.

Just remember to keep your mind open to ways you can use the concept of helping push people in the direction they are already headed in so you can make more money.

That's my "hitch-a-ride" concept. It's much easier to hitch a ride with someone to somewhere they're already going instead of trying to get them to take you where you want to go, which may be in the opposite direction. You'll encounter a lot of resistance that way.

A lot of times, that's what we (as marketers) do. We try to convince people to do things we want them to do (like buy from us) instead of showing them how our products can help them get to the destination they've already picked out in their heads.

"Hitching A Ride" To Success Is Nothing New

Back in 1848 the "California Gold Rush" began. People came from all over the world to claim their share of the wealth. Now you would think that the people who found the most gold were the wealthiest of the time but that isn't exactly true.

The actual fact of the matter is that the people who consistently became rich were the ones who sold tools to those who were mining for gold. People who never found one ounce of gold bought shovels, rugged jeans and other supplies.

Merchants who sold those tools consistently made money no matter how much gold was found.

Selling the tools people need to do something they want to do will always fill your pockets with cash. This concept always works, and it never gets stale like specific marketing strategies.

Try and wrap your mind around the concept and you'll be able to come up with your own techniques to use it with.

Make People Have To Go Through You To Get Where They Want To Go

When you control the tools people need to do whatever it is they want to do, you control the actions they take and that includes how they spend their money. If someone has to go through you to get to their destination faster, you can't help but make money.

You see examples of people selling tools all the time. You just have to pay attention. Notice how many things you can't do unless you pay someone for his or her tool to help you do it.

I Haven't Even Scratched The Surface

There are so many ways to use the concepts I teach that it literally boggles the mind. Spend some time thinking about how you can "hitch a ride" with people who are looking to spend money to get to their destination and I'm sure you can come up with more than a few ideas.

When you see people doing something they want to do, think about ways to get them to pay you to help them do more of it.

By doing that, you won't need tons of specific ideas from me because you will be able to come up with your own. I just wanted you to understand the basic idea of how this works.

Once you understand the basic idea, you'll never be at the mercy of "gurus" constantly trying to peddle specific ideas and strategies on you because you'll understand the big idea behind how and why they work.

If you look at it, all the gurus do is "hitch a ride" on your desire for a better life by giving you what you think you need; the latest "secret" marketing ideas, tips and strategies to give you an edge over the competition. If you think you need something else, they'll sell you whatever it is that you've shown an interest in.

In other words, your major competitors (the people you learn from) are constantly trying to figure out what you want to do so they can sell you ideas, techniques and tools to help you do more of it knowing you will always pay for anything you think will get you closer to achieving whatever goals you've set for yourself.

When you buy from one person over another, the only reason you do is because that person has done a better job (presentation wise) of showing you that what they have to offer will help get you to your goals faster than the other guy.

This idea works when selling any type of product or service. Find out what people want to do (many times this is as easy as asking them) then show them how your product helps them do that.

Always remember that the basis for creating products is to help people do more of something they already want to do. For example, if people want to make more money, instead of simply showing them how, give them an easy way to do it with a minimum amount of effort.

Set everything up for them and allow them to plug into your system and get paid for sending buyers your way.

Or you could create simple products based on hot trends you see and sell the reprint rights to that information allowing people to profit from a trend they're already interested in.

You should never run out of ideas for products so you should never feel bad for selling the rights to something you've created thinking that you just gave away a moneymaking product.

Create something else and keep moving forward.

The biggest thing to remember when you create products that you sell reprint rights to is make sure that those products lead back to your site in some fashion so you can capture the names and email addresses of the people who visit.

The Simple Truth That Will Always Make You Money Whenever You Want Or Need It

Every person who runs across your site has a secret desire. They

want the benefits of what you're offering, but (here's a shocker) they

really don't want to do much to get those benefits.

The most persuasive and profitable product offers are the ones

that make people feel as though they don't have to do much work to

get all the benefits your letter promises.

In other words, if you make your product offers sound too complicated you'll lose most of the orders you could have had.

I'm saying that you should explain your offer in rather simplistic terms that don't scare away potential buyers.

You should always look to make your products and services as pushbutton as you possibly can.

That's especially important with software programs.

No one really cares how your product works. They just want to know

that it does work and how they don't have to do much to get the benefits your product was promised to deliver.

For the most part people are very insecure about their abilities. Even when you show them proof that other people have done exactly

what you're showing them how to do... Most people still hesitate

because they don't believe they can do it.

In other words... you need to put together "systems" people can just plug into and get results from.

Most people don't want to know how to do something. They want someone who does know how to do something to do it for them so they can either promote your something as an affiliate or buy the rights to your something and sell it without having to put in any real work.

Understand this ...

If you have the time and you're willing to do something constructive you will always be in a position to make money from people who want the benefits of doing something without actually having to put in any real work.

That will always be true.

What does that all mean as far as making money?

To continue with my earlier train of thought, I created a special report that shows you how to take autoresponder courses you create and get other people to flood those course with subscribers, but as I've said, people don't want to know how to do that.

What they actually want is for me or you to create a "system" where they can buy the rights to an autoresponder course that is already set up so they can use the technique I outline to get other people to flood that course with subscribers for them so they don't really have to do much. They want the benefits of using the technique without taking any of the time and effort to learn it and set it up for themselves.

For the most part, people complain about FREE detailed instructions on something that actually produces results with a little effort but they would gladly pay $100-$200 or more for a system that uses the very same technique they could have created themselves for free.

Some of that is laziness but mostly it's due to the fact that many people work hard at 9-5 jobs, have a family and other obligations that take up most of the time they would need to put various techniques and strategies they learn into action for themselves.

Both types of people will gladly pay for something that's already done for them so if you're willing to put in a little work for those people you can make as much money as you want.

Some people make obscene amounts of money by doing what I just talked about. They trade a few week's worth of work for $40,000-$50,000+ in bankable profits.

Allen Says of "The Internet Marketing Warriors" wrote something about it in one of his reports along the lines of …

"Any solution you come up with that makes it easy

on people has a 100% better chance of selling than

anything that requires them to work. The majority of

people want things already done, and they will pay

top dollar to have it done for them."

Always keep your brain asking questions. Whenever you learn how to do something, ask yourself and find out if there is a market of people who would pay to have that done for them. You might not always be able to come up with something good but sometimes you will.

The Best Kept Success Secret

It's time you understand that the absolute easiest and most profitable way to get things done in business is to get help.

It's all about the contacts you make.

Trying to make it alone and fighting against the odds is what you've been taught, but it's wrong. You need help.

How often do you take the time to build relationships online?

The answer to that question will determine how far you get.

I constantly search out new friends and business associates because I know that there will come a time when I will need or want their help and vice versa.

When you actively seek out relationships with others in your market you automatically open yourself up to opportunities that the average businessperson would easily miss because they're out of the loop.

Examples:

There are a lot of products I didn't have to buy because their creators who happen to be friends of mine gave me access so that I could help them with any design and marketing strategy questions they had. I have over 15 gigs worth of various digital products I got free.

This also puts me in a position to work with these same marketers on future projects, which is always a good position to be in.

Joint Ventures are extremely easy to get going because I can always contact the people I've worked with in the past to do more deals. Having to constantly search out new people to work with costs you time that you could have been using to make money.

Setting up joint ventures is just a simple matter of sending out a few emails to people who are already used to hearing from me.

There are many services that others routinely pay for that I get for free or at a deeply discounted price because of the contacts I've established over the years.

That's why they'll sometimes perform services for me without the need for money exchanging hands. They know that when my area of expertise is needed... I'll gladly help.

The right relationships mean more money. Having contacts just for the sake of having them is worthless. You need to make the *right* contacts. You need to build relationships with people who can help you get to where you want to be.

But... in order to do that you must have something valuable to offer in return.

There's only so much a friend will help you do. You will need to offer a valuable service in return for the one you want from your contact. That's just the way it works.

If you don't have the money to get things done, then you need to get creative. You don't have to do everything yourself. Search for people who know how to do what you want done and strike up a conversation with them.

There are actually people out there who love to create products, but don't care too much for marketing and people who love marketing and don't care much for creating products.

There are things that you do that other people either don't know

how to or care to do on their own. This is where you step in and form a mutually beneficial relationship.

An added benefit of making the *right* contacts is that even if you can't find someone to do what you need done for free, some of your contacts will know where to get quality work done through "hidden" channels at prices not revealed to just anyone.

You have to be on the "inside" to get this kind of info.

You've got to get it out of your head that everyone is your competitor because competition is not really an issue once you understand that if you're willing to go above and beyond what everyone else is willing to do for their customers, competition is extremely light.

Bottom line: Once you have good contacts in place you can easily get projects off the ground while those who are trying to do everything themselves struggle for months if not years.

It's the difference between having to spend $1,000 to get something done and having your contacts offer to do the exact same work for almost nothing. I guess it really comes down to one question...

"Do you want to put yourself ahead of the competition?"

Don't Bury This Book In The Backyard

I made that mistake for so many years.

Accumulating things can form a habit that gets in the way of you learning from what you have and taking action on it.

How much stuff do you already have buried never again to see the light of day? You probably can't even begin to tell me because collecting and forgetting is an easy and extremely unprofitable thing to do.

I can promise you with 100% certainty that if you don't do anything with the information in this book then it won't help you one little bit. However, if you're the kind of person I think you are, you realize what you now have in front of you.

You have an opportunity to clear your head and regain your focus, but only if you're willing to put consistent effort towards the right things.

What Are The Right Things?

LEVERAGE – Letting other people help you multiply your efforts on any project you create. Never create a project that other people can't help you promote. It just doesn't make sense to do everything on your own when 100's of other people can pour thousands of combined hours into building your business for you.

Have a clear picture in mind ahead of time and incorporate other people and what you need them to do into your overall strategy before you begin. Have a plan to reach your destination.

HITCH-A-RIDE – Look at what other people are doing and think of ways you can profit by helping them do more of it. Nobody cares about what you want unless it happens to coincide with what they want. Stop standing in people's way and instead "push them" towards the goals they're trying to reach.

- - - - -

And stop falling at the feet of "gurus" waiting for them to throw out their leftover "scraps". Pay more attention to what they do and a little less to what they say because intentional or not, a lot of what they say has nothing to do with what they actually do.

Sure they may use the techniques and specific strategies they give you but they're also operating with a bigger picture in mind that they either can't articulate because they don't fully realize what they're doing or simply won't tell the masses.

You are your own leader.

Look to others for guidance but to yourself for the final word on what you should and shouldn't do!

www.ingramcontent.com/pod-product-compliance
Lightning Source LLC
Chambersburg PA
CBHW070627220526
45466CB00001B/112